The Bedside, Bathtub & Armchair Companion to Sherlock Holmes

Dick Riley & Pam McAllister

CONTINUUM • NEW YORK

1999
The Continuum Publishing Company
370 Lexington Avenue
New York, NY 10017

Design by Stefan Killen Design
Printed in the United States of America
Library of Congress Cataloging-in-Publication Data

Riley, Dick.
        The bedside, bathtub & armchair companion to Sherlock Holmes / Dick Riley
& Pam McAllister.
                p.   cm.
        Summary:
        ISBN: 0-8264-1140-1 (alk. paper) – ISBN 0-8264-1116-9 (pbk. : alk. paper)
        1. Doyle, Arthur Conan, Sir, 1859-1930–Characters–Sherlock Holmes.
2. Holmes, Sherlock (Fictitious character)–Miscellanea.   3. Detective and mystery
stories, English–Miscellanea.   4. Private investigators in literature–Miscellanea.
I. McAllister, Pam.   II. Title.
        PR4624.R55   1999
        823'.8–dc21   98-23376
                                        CIP

Contents

Great cesspool and world capital, London's population exceeded that of many nations; the most urbanized, productive, and prosperous city in the world, it ranged from the mansions of Belgravia to the East End where "the tenement houses swelter and reek with the outcasts of Europe."

It was not the Scotland Yard of real life, nor the detectives of fiction, who prefigured Sherlock Holmes. A Scottish physician named Joseph Bell was the real-life inspiration for the great detective, and he established for Conan Doyle a standard of observational skill that Scotland Yard could never seem to meet.

Dozens of actors have portrayed Sherlock Holmes. Some, famous in their time, are now footnotes to theatrical history; others, like John Barrymore and Michael Caine, have gone on to fame in other roles. But William Gillette, Basil Rathbone, and Jeremy Brett defined Holmes for their respective generations.

The portrait of Sherlock Holmes as ascetic and self-denying misreads the evidence. Holmes was an enthusiastic pleasure seeker, even if the things that made him happy weren't everyone's cup of tea.

The British Empire was the predominant geopolitical fact of life not just for the British, but for millions of the world's people. The present and former colonies were also the source of many of Conan Doyle's most "ripping" yarns, from the ancient cities of India to the wilds of the Australian outback and the Great American Desert.

To American readers, one of the most confusing institutions in English life is the peerage–Dukes and Duchesses, Earls and Countesses, Barons and Knights. Here's the explanation of who outranks whom in the Holmes stories, how they are addressed, and the story behind how Holmes's creator became Sir Arthur.

One character in The Sign of the Four *stands to inherit half a million sterling, while the street urchins of the Baker Street Irregulars are happy with a shilling a day. Here's a precise accounting of English money, what it meant in dollars, and what it could buy in Holmes's time.*

Preface

Statement of Faith

Midway through the dramatization of *Peter Pan* (based on the story by Sir Arthur Conan Doyle's friend James M. Barrie) children are prompted to clap their hands if they believe in fairies. Only their heartfelt expressions will keep Tinker Bell alive. It works every time: the children clap their hands and shout into the darkness "I believe! I believe." Can there be any doubt their faithfulness has kept Tink alive all these years?

So too, adult readers around the world and throughout the twentieth century –whether curled comfortably in armchairs, propped up by pillows in our beds, or cautiously reading as we soak in our tubs–have kept the gaslit world of Holmes and Watson alive in our imaginations. How precious the smoke curling around *our* detective's head, how familiar the fog that blankets *our* Baker Street. Oblivious to the shriek of car alarms or jets passing overhead, we hear only the clop of the horses pulling hansoms or Mrs. Hudson's weary tred on the seventeen steps.

Not by clapping our hands, but by cherishing the collections of Conan Doyle's stories–checking them out of libraries, buying them at bookstores, joining with other readers in person or on the Internet to study and revel together–we have kept the beloved duo alive and the game afoot. No flickering flame here; the idiosyncratic sleuth and his amiable amanuensis live on in style and will no doubt survive the millennium. *The Bedside, Bathtub & Armchair Companion to Sherlock Holmes* is the written equivalent of a shout in the dark of the postmodern age–we still believe!

In recognition of the historic Holmes, we have chosen to use the titles and spellings as they first appeared in print and to preserve English rather than American spellings in direct quotations from the Canon.

Sprinkled throughout this book are highlighted quotes by Sherlock Holmes about the art of detective work.

Acknowledgments

Our volume owes a great deal to works by other authors, including, but not exclusively: *A Sherlock Holmes Handbook* by Christopher Redmond (1993, Simon & Pierre, Toronto); *The Annotated Sherlock Holmes* edited by William S. Baring-Gould (1967, Clarkson N. Potter, New York); *A Sherlock Holmes Companion* edited by Peter Haining (1980, Barnes & Noble, New York); *The Life and Times of Sherlock Holmes* by Philip Weller with Christopher Roden (1992, Studio Editions, Ltd., London); *The Encyclopaedia Sherlockiana* by Jack Tracy (1977, Doubleday, New York); and *Encyclopedia Sherlockiana* by Matthew E. Bunson (1994, Macmillan, New York).

A number of other works were helpful in providing background information for the Victorian period, among them *The Oxford Illustrated History of Britain* edited by Kenneth O. Morgan (1984, Oxford University Press, Oxford, England); *London, A Social History* by Roy Porter (1994, Harvard University Press, Cambridge); and *What Jane Austen Ate and Charles Dickens Knew* by Daniel Pool (1993, Touchstone, New York).

We are grateful to the many members of Sherlockian/Holmesian societies around the world who shared their insights with us and encouraged us in our efforts. We also thank the Museum of Modern Art and Tom Rogers of Foto Fantasies for assistance with the illustrations.

Pam thanks her family for their faithful support and owes a debt of gratitude to Cynthia for her friendship, feedback, Internet assistance, and her sense of humor. Dick thanks Marcia for her years of unending encouragement and Ian and Jessa for being who they are. We'd like to thank Evander Lomke, whose patience and attention were critical to the creation of this book. Thanks also to Stefan Killen whose visual imagination helped bring the pages to life.

Dick Riley and Pam McAllister
New York City, July 1998

Imagine Holmes without His Hat:
The Impact of Illustrators

===◦/◦/◦===

Sherlock Holmes is universally recognized by his deerstalker hat. Yet it was an artist, not the author, who first imagined this accessory and attached it to the detective.

That artist, who fashioned the detective the whole world knows by sight, was Sidney Paget. His 356 illustrations for the Sherlock Holmes Canon gave us the beloved Victorian eccentric who lives so vividly in our imaginations. But this was so by accident.

When the editors of *The Strand Magazine* decided to seek an illustrator for Conan Doyle's detective series, they recalled the fine drawings for publications of *Robinson Crusoe* and *Treasure Island* done by an artist whose last name was Paget. There were five Paget brothers, three of them artists. Apparently the editors at *The Strand Magazine* had little of the detective's curiosity or investigative skills, for they failed to ascertain that it was Walter Paget who had rendered the illustrations they admired. Consequently, they commissioned the wrong brother.

If Walter had gotten the job, chances are the world would have had a very different image of the great detective. Walter Paget was known as a real stickler for detail, and it is likely that he would have portrayed Holmes as Watson described him–with a hawklike nose, thin lips, and piercing eyes with dark, heavy brows.

When Sidney Paget (1860-1908) was mistakenly offered the job by the editors of *The Strand Magazine,* his first move was to employ his handsome younger brother Walter as a model, and so it is Walter's face we see, immortalized in the form of the master detective. More than once, readers of *The Strand Magazine,* seeing Walter in a London crowd or party, had occasion to exclaim, "Look, there's Sherlock Holmes!"

Many have suggested that Paget's drawings, of a detective more handsome than his creator ever intended him to be, were at least partly responsible for Holmes's popularity with the readers of the *Strand.* In his biography of Conan Doyle, Charles Higham wrote:

Paget's use of a sexually attractive,

Sidney Paget first depicted Sherlock Holmes wearing a deerstalker in the illustrations for "The Boscombe Valley Mystery."

well-fleshed nineties face and figure paid off handsomely. His image of Sherlock Holmes had hundreds of thousands of young women yearn for this fictional character as they might yearn for a stage actor, and a similar number of men wanted to emulate his flawless tailoring and various forms of headgear. Sherlock Holmes became a star before movies were born, and through no wish of his creator.

In *Memories and Adventures,* Conan Doyle himself commented on the benefit of Paget's more generous conception of Holmes:

He had, as I imagined him, a thin razor-like face with a great hawks-bill of a nose, and two small eyes, set close together on either side of it. It chanced, however, that Sidney Paget had a younger brother who served him as a model. The handsome

Walter took the place of the more powerful, but uglier, Sherlock, and perhaps from the point of view of my lady readers it was as well.

The first time Holmes wore a deerstalker was in Paget's illustrations for "The Boscombe Valley Mystery." Sidney's daughter Winifred later explained in an essay:

> It was during the time that my father lived in the country that he wore that surely now most famous of all hats–the deerstalker; and the fact that he liked it and found it comfortable inspired him to depict Holmes wearing it on so many occasions.

Holmes's famous deerstalker was not depicted by Paget *many* times, yet those few drawings caught and held the public imagination. We see Holmes and Watson on the railway coach, Holmes, in his deerstalker, leaning eagerly toward his bowler-hatted traveling companion. We see Holmes's long body stretched in the grass where he is carefully inspecting the ground looking for clues, the brim of his deerstalker neatly shading his eyes. Or we see the deerstalker frozen in midair, caught in the moment of tumbling into Reichenbach Falls while Holmes wrestles with Moriarty on the slippery path.

Clearly the hat appealed to Conan Doyle, for a year after it first appeared in Paget's drawings, in "The Adventure of Silver Blaze," the author described Holmes's face, "framed in his ear-flapped travelling cap"– his closest reference to a deerstalker.

The first published illustration of Sherlock Holmes was by D. H. Friston for Beeton's Christmas Annual, *1887.*

Paget had drawn his first depiction of Sherlock Holmes in 1891, when he was thirty-one years old. Unfortunately, the artist's gift to the world came to an abrupt end in 1908 when he died at age forty-seven after years of chest complaints.

Paget was not the first illustrator of Holmes. That distinction belongs to D. H. Friston, whose two pictures of the new detective appear in *Beeton's Annual* with the first publication of *A Study in*

Had Charles read his son's story? It seems unlikely. His Holmes is probably the only bearded one in existence, and in his drawings the detective's shoulders are so rounded they almost don't exist. The nose, too, far from being "hawk-like," is almost nonexistent. In fact, Holmes and the other characters drawn by Charles Doyle all look weak and strange if not downright demented. Conan Doyle was a Victorian gentleman who would not have publicly disparaged this artwork; we can only imagine his true feelings at his father's fiasco. The greater puzzle is why the publishers went ahead with illustrations of such meager quality. One commentator, Walter Klinefelter, wrote, "Charles Doyle definitely achieved the all-time low in the portraiture of the man. Mere words are too ineffectual to describe this Holmes."

At least three other illustrators tried their hand at sketching the detective/doctor duo, before Paget gave the world the Holmes we all know as depicted in the first half of the Canon.

Most notable of the illustrators to complete the second half of Holmesian portraiture was the American, Frederic Dorr Steele. At that time, the tall, suave, eccentric American actor, William Gillette, had donned the deerstalker, successfully capturing the public imagination as a living, breathing Sherlock Holmes on stage. Steele wisely made the decision to base his conception of the fictional detective on the actor. In an essay, Steele explained;

> Everybody agreed that Mr. Gillette was the ideal Sherlock Holmes, and it was inevitable that I should copy him. So I made my models look like him,

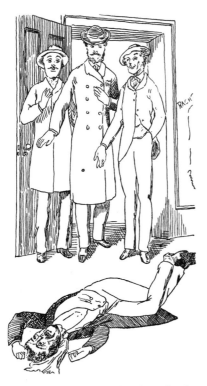

Arthur Conan Doyle's asylum-bound father Charles drew this illustration of a bearded Holmes for "A Study in Scarlet."

Scarlet. To our eyes, Friston's Holmes is an outrage. His head and hands appear small, almost feminine, his sideburns are ridiculously long, and his figure is plump, dwarfed by the oversized coat. On his head appears a strange, rounded hat. This Holmes looks nothing like the detective we know.

Modern readers have even more cause for alarm when viewing the artwork solicited in 1888 by Ward, Lock & Company for the first publication of *A Study in Scarlet* in book form. The artist was none other than Conan Doyle's alcoholic, asylum-bound father, Charles.

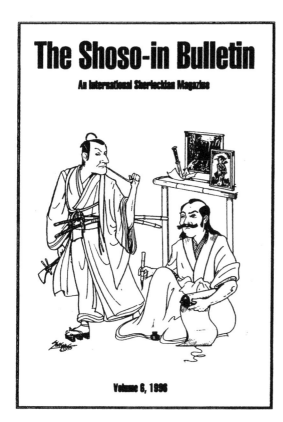

Left: Cover illustration of a Japanese Holmes and Watson for the Shoso-in Bulletin *by Stu Shiffman.*

Below: Logo for the Winston & Holmes, billed as Toronto's "foremost tobacconist."

Bottom: This personalized advertisement by the Fern Home Furnishers, Inc. of Syracuse, NY, c. 1925 depicts Holmes and Watson investigating the whereabouts of a lapsed customer.

and even in two or three instances used photographs of him in my drawings. . . . I did not see the play until a later revival, some time after my first series of drawings was completed. Mr. Gillette was good enough to ask me back to his dressing room and to chat with me about our mutual friend.

According to veteran Sherlockian Christopher Redmond, the Gillette/ Steele influence was responsible for the addition of Holmes's curved pipe.

It is generally thought that the curved pipe now associated with Holmes, but not mentioned in the Canon or seen in early illustrations, was introduced by Gillette, who found that his speeches were more audible over it, and his face more visible, than through a straight pipe.

Just as the deerstalker was the invention of Sidney Paget, the curved pipe, introduced by Gillette, was taken up by Steele and set permanently in place in the public's imagination. Over time, the curved bowl became flared, and today the detective is frequently pictured smoking a calabash pipe.

Steele's drawings for *Collier's Weekly* rival Paget's for their faithful revelations of the master detective, his moods and temperament, his gestures and interactions. Steele's craggy Holmes was drawn with bold, clean lines. By dropping fussy detail, he brought Holmes into the twentieth century, yet somehow managed to capture that golden time "where it is always 1895."

An illustration by Steele.

The work of the early artists, Paget and Steele, shaped the initial image of the detective, but did not define it for all time. Sherlock Holmes was a character destined for greatness. His likeness has been rendered in comic books and Sunday cartoons, and has been used extensively in advertising to sell everything from tobacco to home furnishings.

It is a testament to his universality that he has, at times, transcended, not only his age and culture, but his race as well. The cover of one international Sherlockian journal, published in 1996 shows a lanky Asian Holmes in Japanese garb, with the scribe, Watson, kneeling at his feet holding scroll and brush. On the mantle is a picture of kimono-clad Irene Adler, to Holmes "always *the* woman."

Living a Victorian Life

———✦✦✦———

So near and yet so far. . . . Life in Victorian London a century ago was in many ways very near our own–and in most important ways nearer to our lives today than it was to the London a century before its own time.

Electric and gas lighting, steam power, the railroad, the subway, modern baths and toilets, even the telephone–all these were present, and in places and times widespread in Victorian and Edwardian years. Nor have styles of dress, particularly men's business clothing, changed dramatically since Holmes's time.

A man of business in Holmes's era could walk down a street in modern London and seem no more than quaint. The business attire of a 1790 gentleman, complete with tricorn hat, wig, and hose, strolling down the Strand would have seemed comical even to Holmes's generation, much less our own.

The urbanization of society, the expansion of wealth and knowledge, the transformative power of technology, all made Victorian times much more like ours than like the societies that had gone before.

Victorian England, no less than our own era, was full of intellectual turmoil. While Einstein's theories were not published until after the turn of the century, Darwin's and even Freud's were acquiring prominence, shaking basic assumptions about human nature and human society. Long-held notions of social class were beginning to change, political reform had extended the vote to hundreds of thousands of men, and the drive for female suffrage was heating up enormously.

But there were also significant differences from our lives today.

The Lack of a Servant Problem

The Holmes stories are full of references to servants, from the butlers who play major roles in *The Hound of the Baskervilles*, "The Adventure of the Musgrave Ritual," and "The Adventure of the 'Gloria Scott'" to pageboys who open doors and fetch cabs. The female

Servants played an important role in Victorian life.

In 1881 an estimated 2,000,000 people, or fully 15 percent of the British labor force, were employed as personal servants. So low were servants' wages that even families we would consider closer to poverty than respectability could afford to have at least one, generally a girl from ranks even poorer than their own who slaved and slept in what passed for the family's kitchen.

Middle-class families would have a cook and a couple of maids. The number of servants rose in general with the funds and prominence of the household, so that a major London mansion or great country estate would include a battalion of footmen, coachmen, gardeners, grooms, housemaids, scullery maids, and others.

Despite the fact that Reginald Musgrave is a bachelor, his estate, Hurlstone Manor, site of "The Musgrave Ritual," has a butler, a cook, eight maids, two footmen, and a boy, while the gardens and stables, in addition, have their own staffs. "In the pheasant months I usually have a house-party, so that it would not do to be short-handed," he explains to Holmes.

They were necessary because the Victorian era had little in the way of labor-saving devices. Every meal that was prepared, every dish washed and rewashed, every piece of clothing laundered and ironed, was done by hand. Unlike a modern car, which can sit unused and ignored for days or weeks at a time, a horse had to be fed, watered, exercised, and cleaned up after every day. Wood or coal had to be taken up to every fireplace every day in season, and ashes brought back down.

Butlers and housekeepers at major

characters range from housekeepers to ladies' maids to kitchen help like the Watson's Mary Jane, mentioned in "A Scandal in Bohemia," whose ineptitude is such that she has all but ruined Dr. Watson's shoes in the effort to clean them.

Servants are always in the background, if not the foreground of the Canon, because that was their position in Victorian life.

estates administered large operations and significant budgets. But they were still servants, even if like Brunton at Hurlstone Manor they had held more middle-class jobs, such as teacher, in previous lives (he was referred to as Brunton as a mark of respect; servants of lesser rank were referred to by their first names).

Governesses like Miss Violet Hunter in "The Adventure of the Copper Beeches" occupied a more ambiguous place. Governesses were typically middle class in origin, or even upper-class young women whose families had fallen on hard times. They were not exactly servants, but not exactly family either.

Going Outside

Particularly in cities, we identify the automobile as a key factor in environmental decline. But among its original selling points was its potential to improve the urban environment.

Seafarers and country visitors to the nineteenth-century European city noticed first of all the odor of horses. The cleanup job that occupied the rich man's groom at his stable every day was multiplied by a factor of thousands on the streets of London—and the city cleanup was done irregularly. The bonnets and veils worn by Victorian ladies were more than a fashion statement. They helped shield them from thrown-up manure (or in dry weather a powdered airborne version) that arose from the city's streets.

> **"It is my belief, Watson, founded upon my experience, that the lowest and vilest alleys in London do not present a more dreadful record of sin than does the smiling and beautiful countryside."**
> —*The Adventure of the Copper Beeches*

Sewers were not necessarily available either, particularly until the end of the nineteenth century, while the atmosphere and waterways of London were poisoned by the effluent of thousands of tanneries, breweries, gas, and chemical plants. In 1858 the odor from the Thames led to the adjournment of Parliament, which could not meet because of "the great stink," although sheets soaked with lime had been hung in the windows of the Houses.

For hundreds of years London had been susceptible to fogs, reportedly so impenetrable at times that people could literally not see their hands in front of their faces. In a number of stories Watson reports fog so thick that windows across Baker Street were "dark, shapeless blurs," and in "The Adventure of the Bruce-Partington Plans" the buildings themselves were invisible (the lack of visibility contributing to delays in discovering the murder of one of the story's characters).

An often-noted peculiarity of the London fog was that it had a yellow cast, though Watson also describes it as a "greasy brown swirl . . . condensing in oily drops upon the windowpane." The average Victorian home burned coal as a heating fuel, and this was thought to be a principal culprit.

Getting Around

Horses and carriages in Holmes's time were expensive and time-consum-

Visitors to the city noticed the odor of horses.

ing luxuries, particularly in the cities. Middle-class people could rent them when absolutely necessary, but in this era it was not thought remarkable that even the well-to-do got around London by foot.

In "The Adventure of the Resident Patient" Watson says of himself and Holmes, "For three hours we strolled about together, watching the ever changing kaleidoscope of life as it ebbs and flows through Fleet Street and the Strand."

But given the distances involved and the degree of urgency that was so often

> **"There is a wonderful sympathy and freemasonry among horsy men. Be one of them, and you will know all that there is to know."**
> —*A Scandal in Bohemia*

part of Holmes's cases, he and Watson often had to rely on cabs and hired coaches.

As late as the eighteenth century and even the early nineteenth the rich had traveled on horseback or in litters. But the paving of streets had encouraged the growth of carriages and coaches. Public transport consisted for a long time of the discarded coaches of the rich being pressed into service for a few more years before they completely disintegrated.

Just as we have sedans, station wag-

Sir Henry Baskerville took a train from Paddington Station to Dartmoor in The Hound of the Baskervilles. Credit: Illustrated London News, *July 8, 1854.*

ons, and sports cars, the nineteenth-century rider had landaus, broughams, and growlers (said to have been named by the sound of their steel wheels on the streets).

But when time was of the essence Holmes and Watson preferred the hansom, a lightweight, two-wheeled one-horse vehicle whose driver sat or stood at the back, partially above the cab. The hansom, however, only had room for two people, and little or no luggage.

"You have splashes on the left sleeve and shoulder of your coat," Holmes remarks to Watson. "Had you sat in the centre of a hansom you would probably have had no splashes and if you had they would certainly have been symmet-

rical. Therefore it is clear that you sat at the side. Therefore it is equally clear that you had a companion."

On the other hand, when Holmes and Watson join Miss Mary Morstan on a potentially dangerous errand in *The Sign of the Four,* the carriage they rely on is a four-wheeler, because the three of them, plus their mysterious guide, could never fit into a single hansom cab.

The Railroad

No technology changed the face of daily life in the nineteenth century as extensively as did the revolution in transportation. Railroads propelled by steam began running in Great Britain about 1830 and by 1870 England had more than 13,000 miles of track, a very significant amount for a nation its size.

English railroads were at first largely confined to intercity service, and tended to terminate at stations on the fringes of metropolitan areas. Each line was a separate private company and, while there was some cooperation, each tended to have its own station. Thus we see Holmes and Watson, who travel by train in many of the stories, going to different stations depending on their destination: Paddington for many points west, Euston and King's Cross for generally northerly journeys, Waterloo for many points south and west.

Without the speed and efficiency of the railroad at bringing in food and necessities, London and other English cities could never have developed into their present size. In addition the railroads, particularly when forced by the government to run one very low-fare (parliamentary) train each day along their lines, made travel possible for hundreds of thousands of people who previously could expect to leave their county, or even their parish, only a few times in their lives.

The underground railway opened in London in 1863 in an effort to reduce London's mammoth traffic congestion. The line ran between Paddington and the City, or financial district, and was gradually extended and similar lines were opened during the time covered by the Holmes stories. Holmes and Watson take the Underground in "The Red-Headed League," and in "The Bruce-Partington Plans" the body of young

Cadogan West is found beside the tracks of an Underground station. (An important story point hinges on the fact that, while it is called the Underground, the trains run, like the New York City subway, partially in trenches rather than exclusively in tunnels.)

Communications

Telegraphy was introduced into England in the middle of the nineteenth century, and by Holmes's time it was established in the major cities, not just for long-distance communications, but also for intracity messages, especially useful given London's expansion.

Telegraph offices were common all over London by Holmes's time, and telegrams play a role in cases as varied as "The Sign of the Four," "Wisteria Lodge," "The Devil's Foot," "The Bruce-Partington Plans," and "The Disappearance of Lady Frances Carfax." Telegrams would be conveyed to the sending offices by servants,

Telegraph offices were common all over London.

and from the receiving offices by commissionaires or messenger boys.

By the 1890s home delivery of the mail (the "post") was virtually universal in England, and many of Holmes's cases start out with letters, from "A Scandal in Bohemia" to "The Problem of Thor Bridge."

But Holmes preferred, in addition to the speed of the telegram, the economy of expression that its payment-by-the-word imposed on correspondents. Holmes "has never been known to write when a telegram would serve" recalls Watson in "The Adventure of the Devil's Foot."

He was even less enamored of the telephone. The first telephone exchange opened in London in 1879, but it is not until the late adventures, such as "The Three Garridebs" and "The Illustrious Client," that a telephone appears at Baker Street.

When letters, the telegraph or the telephone were inadequate, Holmes could rely on the "agony column" or personal advertisements in London newspapers. In "The Copper Beeches" Holmes has been, by Watson's account, "dipping continuously into the advertisement columns of a succession of newspapers"; it was the agony column of the *Times* that he was reading when Watson arrived with his patient for a consultation in "The Adventure of the Engineers' Thumb"; in "The Adventure of the Red Circle" Holmes clipped the columns from a number of newspapers including the *Daily Gazette*; he used an advertisement in the agony column to try to find a cabdriver who might have picked up a fare in Whitehall in "The Adventure of the Naval Treaty."

Despite his disdain–"What a chorus of groans, cries and bleatings"–Holmes found the agony column useful, even necessary. "Surely the most valuable hunting ground that ever was given to a student of the unusual."

CAPSULE

A Study in Scarlet

First Publication:

Beeton's Christmas Annual, November 1887

Principal Predicament:

The body of Enoch Drebber has been discovered in an abandoned house. Though there is an abundance of blood in the room, there is no wound on the dead American. His immaculate collar and cuffs and well-brushed top hat all bespeak wealth, but why did he die with such an expression of horror on his apelike face? On the wall, in blood-red letters, is scrawled RACHE, the German word for "revenge." And then there is the wedding ring, meant for a woman's finger, but found with the body. As he leaves the crime scene, Holmes informs the Scotland Yard detectives that the murderer is a tall man with a red face, long fingernails, and square-toed boots.

Notable Feature:

In this novella, young Stamford escorts Dr. Watson to the chemical laboratory of St. Bartholomew's Hospital where he utters the famous words, "Dr. Watson, Mr. Sherlock Holmes." After a perfunctory, "How are you?" the world's first consulting detective speaks his immortal words, "You have been in Afghanistan, I perceive." Soon after, we venture for the first time into the 221-B Baker Street flat and then—the game's afoot.

Sherlock Holmes and Dr. Watson are introduced in this early illustration by George Hutchinson.

Quotable Quote:

Holmes: *"To a great mind, nothing is little."*

Oddities and Discrepancies:

Where is Watson's war wound? In this story Watson writes that, while serving in the Afghan war, he was "struck on the shoulder by a Jezail bullet, which shattered the bone and grazed the subclavian artery." But in *The Sign of the Four,* he nurses his wounded *leg,* explaining, "I had had a Jezail bullet through it some time before, and though it did not prevent me from walking it ached wearily at every change of the weather."

The Sign of the Four

First Publication:

Lippincott's Monthly Magazine, February 1890

Principal Predicament:

". . . in rushed a dozen dirty and ragged little street arabs."

Holmes is aroused from his drug-induced stupor by the excitement of an exotic new case as presented by Miss Mary Morstan, a "well-gloved" blue-eyed blond with a sweet expression. She tells a strange tale. Ten years earlier, she'd received word from her father, an officer in an Indian regiment, that he had returned to England and wanted to meet her in London. Motherless and with no other relative in England, she was eager to be reunited with her father and went at once to London, but her father had vanished and has never been heard of since. There is more. Mary had responded to an ad in *The Times* that asked specifically for her address. Since that time, once a year, she has received through the post a small cardboard box containing a very large, lustrous pearl. That very morning, she received a letter from an "unknown friend," advising her to be "at the third pillar from the left outside the Lyceum Theater at seven o'clock." Holmes, upon hearing the details of the predicament, says, "Well, really, this is a very pretty little mystery!" Indeed.

Notable Feature:

The story opens with a shockingly detailed description of Holmes taking up his hypodermic syringe, rolling up his shirt-cuff, finding a prominent vein in his sinewy forearm, scarred with puncture marks, and injecting himself with a seven-percent solution of cocaine. On a happier note, we meet the Baker Street Irregulars, the street urchins who assist Holmes, and we learn a lot about Watson who, in the course of the story, falls in love.

Quotable Quote:

Holmes: *"I am the last and highest court of appeal in detection."*

CAPSULE

A Scandal in Bohemia

First Publication:

The Strand Magazine, July 1891

Principal Predicament:

In just three days, the betrothal of the King of Bohemia to the second daughter of the King of Scandinavia will be publicly proclaimed. His Majesty–a Hercules in fur-trimmed boots and gaudy garb–is worried. He's sure his bride-to-be, who is "the very soul of delicacy," would not appreciate the compromising picture and love letters his jilted ex-lover, Irene Adler, threatens to send. Adler is a diminutive adventuress and famed operatic contralto with a soul of steel, the face a man might die for, and a mind so clever it leaves the unflappable Holmes dazed. The worried King has twice had Adler waylaid and searched, to no avail, nor is the bitter beauty likely to trust her banker or lawyer with the damning evidence. In the course of uncovering its hiding place, the detective dons two disguises so effective his very soul seems to change. But then, someone else dons an effective disguise too.

Notable Feature:

Watson opens with, "To Sherlock Holmes she is always *the* woman." Indeed, in this story, Holmes is outsmarted by "the daintiest thing under a bonnet on this planet."

Quotable Quote:

Holmes: *"I am lost without my Boswell."*

Oddities and Discrepancies

Illustration from a Spanish publication of "A Scandal in Bohemia." Credit: Ana Capitaine, illustrator

(1) What has happened to Mrs. Hudson, the faithful landlady of the Baker Street flat? It's Mrs. Turner who brings the tray and serves the "simple fare." (2) Why the big rush to get to the church before noon? This adventure took place in March 1888. In May 1886 English law had been changed, extending the legal period for a marriage to 3 p.m. English law also required not one, but two witnesses to a marriage ceremony. Where was the second witness?

CAPSULE

The Red-Headed League

First Publication:

The Strand Magazine, August 1891

Principal Predicament:

Jabez Wilson, an obese and gullible pawnbroker with blazing red hair, arrives at Baker Street with an amazing story. The eccentric American million-aire, Ezekiah Hopkins, died and left his fortune to benefit a philanthropic orga-nization, the League of Red-Headed Men. Prompted by a newspaper ad about a job opening at the League and encouraged to apply by his cheap but handy assistant, Vincent Spaulding, Wilson pushed through a throng of red-headed contenders to the front of the line at the Fleet Street office. To his amazement, Mr. Wilson was chosen to fill the vacancy. His job assignment--copy the *Encyclopaedia Britannica*. He was very happy in his position until the League was abruptly dissolved. Holmes is at once amused and alarmed. "I think that it is possible that graver issues hang from it than might at first sight appear," he muses. Before the game is up, Holmes and Watson must sit in pitch darkness beside Mr. Jones of Scotland Yard and Mr. Merryweather, a bank director, wait-ing for the light.

Notable Feature:

Sherlock Holmes uses his favorite weapon--a loaded hunting crop.

Quotable Quote:

Holmes: *"It is quite a three-pipe problem."*

Oddities and Discrepancies

When did this story take place? In his fretful opening narrative, Mr. Jabez Wilson presents a newspaper clipping advertising a job for a red-headed man. The clipping is from *The Morning Chronicle* dated April 27, 1890–"just two months ago," notes Watson. This statement would place the story in June, but Wilson concludes his narrative by presenting to Holmes the white cardboard sign he'd found on the office door: "THE RED-HEADED LEAGUE IS DISSOLVED. October 9, 1890."

Above: *". . . there was nothing remarkable about the man save his blazing red head, and the expression of extreme chagrin and discontent upon his features."*

Steel True, Blade Straight—
Arthur Conan Doyle

—◦◦◦—

"A dignified spinster with syphilis" was how one biographer described the city of Edinburgh, Scotland, into which Arthur Conan Doyle (hereafter referred to as ACD) was born on May 22, 1859. It was an age of luxury and extravagance for the Edinburgh elite to whom Scottish thrift was a scorned memory and social conscience a joke. As its resources were squandered, the city festered like an open sore. Glue and tanning factories spewed a nauseating stench, and gutters overflowed with raw sewage. With only a few gaslit streets, most of the city lay in darkness, plagued by crime, poverty, and disease. ACD was born to the dark side of this divided city and, at age six, wrote his first story– about a man eaten alive by a tiger.

On his father's side, the family tree was resplendent with talented and accomplished artists descended from a long line of Irish Catholic gentry. At the head was his Irish grandfather, John Doyle, an acclaimed political caricaturist, known to the public by his cipher "HB." (ACD's readers would later find these same initials inscribed in a tell-tale hat in "The Adventure of Blue Carbuncle.")

Grandfather Doyle had five sons, four of whom were artistically gifted. ACD's Uncle Henry became the director of the National Gallery of Ireland. Uncle James was known for his portraits. Uncle Francis created detailed miniatures before his death at age fifteen. Uncle Richard was the most skilled and successful. A painter of fairies and elves, he designed the cover of *Punch* that would be retained for over a hundred years. Uncle Richard also had a noteworthy distraction: in good times and bad, when he needed to brood, he picked up a violin and fiddled absentmindedly.

Into this line of talented sons came ACD's father, the woefully less talented Charles Altamont Doyle, called by one biographer "the unlucky youngest son of a remarkable family." (The name Altamont would figure significantly in "His Last Bow," as the alias used by

Arthur Conan Doyle, from an engraving in a 1900 edition of The Refugees.

Sherlock Holmes in his guise as an Irish-American spy.) Plagued by epilepsy and depression, Charles was never able to move his wife and children out of cramped, shabby, dark rooms. A second-rate architect and designer, he supplemented his income by sketching criminal trials and illustrating children's books. In his melancholy moods, he painted morbid watercolors. ACD later hung two of these, "The Ghost Coach" and "The Haunted House," on the walls of his consulting room in Southsea. Alcoholism undermined what little skill and vitality Charles had, and, in 1883, he was committed to a mental hospital.

Mary Foley Doyle, ACD's mother, affectionately known as "the Ma'am," survived in this bleak landscape by obsessively reciting a romantic version of her own family tree. Fact and wishful thinking were loosely bound together in her lineage of noble ancestors. Recounting tales of chivalry and honor sustained her as she nurtured her children.

At age nine, ACD was sent to a Catholic prep school in Lancashire. After two years he graduated to Stonyhurst, a famous school run by the Jesuits, which claimed ownership of a thorn from Christ's crown, the thumb of a martyr, and the shinbone of a saint. Life at both schools was grim and austere, featuring meager meals, long prayers, unheated bathrooms, and constant surveillance by the brothers to prevent "immoral behavior." Corporal punishment was generously meted out.

ACD endured the harsh atmosphere bravely, excelling on the playing field and occasionally leading other boys into "escapades" to flirt with girls or buy tobacco. He was a voracious reader, devouring works by Sir Walter Scott, Oliver Wendell Holmes, and novels depicting the American wilderness by the Irish writer/fur trapper Mayne Reid. He exercised his imagination and entertained his schoolmates at Stonyhurst with tales of terror or adventure that kept his listeners enthralled.

His world expanded significantly during the Christmas of 1874 when the fifteen-year-old storyteller visited his famous Uncle Richard in London. There, ACD indulged his fascination with the macabre; he and his uncle visited the Chamber of Horrors in Madame Tussaud's Wax-Works on Baker Street, took in *Hamlet* at the Lyceum, and dallied over the instruments of torture on display at the Tower of London.

To improve his German language skills, he spent much of the next year at a school in western Austria where he joined the school band, choosing for his instrument the bombardon horn. About this bass tuba, called the largest brass horn in existence, ACD allowed, "Blowing it is splendid work for the chest." While in Austria, ACD began to read the stories of the French writer Émile Gaboriau as well as those of Edgar Allan Poe, whose influence he would later both admit and deny, honor and discredit. Before returning to Scotland, he spent several weeks with his great uncle and godfather, Michael Conan, in Paris.

In 1877 ACD entered Edinburgh University to study medicine. He was chosen to be the outpatient clerk for Dr. Joseph Bell, a surgeon who gave lectures at the Edinburgh Infirmary, and who was famous for his powers of observation.

Now a brawny young man with a booming voice, ACD was not happy at the university, which he described as "a great unsympathetic machine." He was a young man in need of adventure, so he took a job as ship's surgeon on a whaling cruise and sailed the Arctic Ocean for seven months. He proved popular for his boxing skills and storytelling, and he joined his crewmates in harpooning whales and butchering seals.

Within months after his return to

Louise ("Touie") Doyle, ACD's first wife, with their first child, Mary, 1893.

England and went into partnership with a former classmate from Edinburgh University, the shady George Budd. Dr. Budd drew people to his practice with free consultations, promised instant cures, and then charged exorbitant fees for his potions. ACD's mother was appalled and warned her son that his friend was a quack. The partnership ended abruptly on a sour note.

Free of this unscrupulous entanglement, ACD rented the house next to the Baptist Church in the resort town of Southsea, a suburb of Portsmouth, and invited his nine-year-old brother Innes to live with him. ACD put his name on the door and waited for patients. To pass the time in those lean days, he attended séances, walked along the ocean front, and wrote stories.

In the spring of 1885 a Gloucester widow, on holiday in Portsmouth with her son Jack and daughter Louise, appealed to the doctor for help. Jack was feverish and shivering. ACD diagnosed cerebral meningitis and, a few days later, witnessed Jack's death. He consoled the grieving family, and, as he did, he became increasingly infatuated with the dead boy's sister. Louise ("Touie") Hawkins was sweet and uncomplicated. At the beginning of August they were married.

The next year, in March 1886, ACD wrote *A Study in Scarlet*, in which he conjured up the pacing detective and

the university, he again went to sea as a surgeon, this time aboard a cargo ship headed for Africa. Unlike the first voyage, however, this was a nightmare trip that brought less adventure than disaster: typhoid fever, a shark attack, a shipboard fire. The beleaguered ship returned to London in January 1882.

Doctor A. Conan Doyle

It was time for ACD to make his way in the world, but the transition was not an easy one for him or his relatives. He shocked his family when he became disillusioned with Roman Catholicism and began to read tracts advocating spiritualism.

He moved to Plymouth in southwest

soft-hearted scribe, a duo destined for a global audience. At first the detective was to be named either Sherringford or Sherrinford Holmes, not Sherlock. Although it is believed that he settled on Sherlock entirely at random, some have speculated that ACD was aware of William Sherlock (1641-1707), the dean of St. Paul's, who had written *A Practical Discourse Concerning Death*. On the other hand, Sherlock was the name of a prominent landowning family in the Ireland of ACD's ancestors. Then too, ACD once said in an interview, "I made thirty runs [at cricket] against a bowler by the name of Sherlock, and I always had a kindly feeling for the name."

As for the name Holmes, again, speculation abounds. We know that ACD was enamored of Oliver Wendell Holmes. As a student, he'd saved his lunch money to purchase his books and later wrote, "Never have I so known and loved a man whom I had never seen. . . . It was one of the ambitions of my lifetime to look into his face, but by the irony of Fate I arrived in his native city just in time to lay a wreath on his newly turned grave."

Nor did the name of Dr. John Watson immediately suggest itself. Instead, ACD toyed with Ormond Sacker as the name of the narrator for his tales, but this name, he decided, sounded "too dandified." He settled on Watson's name, thinking, perhaps, of his friend James Watson of Edinburgh who had come to Southsea in 1883 and was a fellow member of the Southsea Literary and Scientific Society.

> "I never guess. It is a shocking habit— destructive to the logical faculty."
> —*The Sign of the Four*

A Study in Scarlet was twice rejected before being published in "a shilling shocker," *Beeton's Christmas Annual* in 1887. ACD sold all rights to the story for £25. Mildly acknowledged by the critics, the story was published in book form in 1888, with cartoonish illustrations of a bearded Sherlock Holmes drawn by ACD's asylum-bound father.

British readers were ready for Sherlock Holmes, indeed craved him. Daily, their newspaper headlines screamed of Jack the Ripper, who confounded the best efforts of the police. The population longed for insight, competence, and cool, blade-sharp logic.

ACD, however, had other needs. He aspired to be the author of historical novels, books that not only entertained but instructed, writing projects that would satisfy his thirst for serious scholarship and political comment. His first such attempt, *Micah Clarke,* set in the seventeenth century during Monmouth's Rebellion, was rejected by a number of publishers until it was finally accepted and appeared in print in February 1889, shortly after the birth of his first child, Mary Louise Conan Doyle. Both the baby and the book were received enthusiastically.

Encouraged, ACD immersed himself in a study of the Middle Ages toward the writing of his next novel, *The White Company*. The thirty-year-old doctor-turned-author summered in a cottage on Emory Down in the New Forest, taking with him a small library of books on medieval history. His research was interrupted, however, by an auspicious invitation.

Joseph Marshall Stoddart, the new manager of the American *Lippincott's Monthly Magazine,* hosted a dinner party on August 30th at London's Langham Hotel, at which two fledgling writers were wined and dined. By the end of the evening, ACD and Oscar Wilde were commissioned to write for the magazine. Wilde's contract resulted in his celebrated story "The Picture of Dorian Gray," and the outcome of ACD's agreement was his second Holmes story, *The Sign of the Four,* published the following year in February 1890.

When this commitment was out of the way, ACD was happily back to work on *The White Company,* creating characters against the background of fourteenth century England and France, pausing only to enjoy the baby and to grieve the death of his sister Annette. In July he cried out, "That's done it!" and threw his pen across the room where its ink splashed across the light blue wallpaper.

Having completed what his editor called "the greatest historical novel since *Ivanhoe,*" ACD grew restless. For the remaining months of 1890 and for part of 1891, ACD erratically explored various options in his medical career. In the space of a few months, he traveled to Berlin to investigate a fantastical claim by a headline-grabbing bacteriologist. He then halfheartedly studied ophthalmology in Vienna where, struggling with medical terminology in German, he also knocked off a novelette and figure-skated with his wife.

In a last, bold attempt to keep one foot in the world of medicine, ACD moved his family to London and hung out a shingle advertising his services as an eye specialist. It is said that he had not one patient. This was the world's good fortune, for, with all that time on his hands, ACD concentrated on writing stories. The would-be doctor peopled his empty office with fictional characters. When a severe bout of influenza knocked the wind out of ACD, he did a quick reevaluation of his life and came to a remarkable conclusion–he would be a writer, full-time.

> I saw how foolish I was to waste my literary earnings in keeping up an oculist's room in Wimpole Street, and I determined with a wild rush of joy to cut the painter and to trust for ever to my power of writing. I remember in my delight taking the handkerchief which lay upon the coverlet in my enfeebled hand and tossing it up to the ceiling in my exultation. I should at last be my own master.

Within weeks, ACD closed up shop and moved his family to a villa in South Norwood, a London suburb. "A Scandal in Bohemia," which he had submitted in April to the tremendously popular new literary magazine, *The Strand,* was published in the July 1891 issue, accompanied by the illustrations of one Sidney Paget.

The Sherlock Holmes Sensation

Almost overnight, Sherlock Holmes became a household name throughout London. ACD wrote the stories quickly, effortlessly, often while entertaining friends. He paid little attention to continuity and detail; seasons sometimes changed overnight, old war wounds moved from one part of the body to another. The readers didn't care. They simply wanted more of Holmes and Watson–and they got it.

August, September, October, November. When the stack of manuscripts ran low, the publishers hurriedly renegotiated, agreeing to pay the author £50 for each story instead of £35. Circulation of *The Strand* had reached half a million for one reason–a hunger and thirst for the Sherlock Holmes stories featured there.

Now ACD found himself in an odd position. His self-contained serial detective stories were so successful that he felt trapped by them. The public's appetite was insatiable. There was no escape. To make matters worse, ACD had a low opinion of detective stories. He longed to be taken seriously as the author of historical fiction. Many years later he would write, "All things find their level, but I believe that if I had never touched Holmes, who has tended to obscure my higher work, my position in literature would at the present moment be a more commanding one."

ACD wanted a break from the relentless deadlines demanded of *The Strand* in order to work on his next historical novel, *The Refugees.* He also needed time to satisfy his need for playing tennis, soccer, and cricket, and riding a tandem tricycle about town with his wife.

After writing the eleventh story in *The Strand* series, ACD wrote to his mother, "I think of slaying Holmes in the last and winding him up for good and all. He takes my mind from better things." The Ma'am, by now a Holmes enthusiast, absolutely forbade it.

To satisfy his craving for more substantial work, ACD took time in December 1891 to work on *The Refugees* and completed the book in the new year. In February 1892 he wrote to his mother, "They have been bothering me for more Sherlock Holmes tales." ACD made an offer he hoped and believed would be refused–that he be paid one thousand pounds for the next set of stories. To his amazement and dismay, the publishers agreed.

By now, ACD had developed confidence in his identity as a writer, and that identity was reinforced by invitations to socialize in the middle echelons of London literary society. He attended the afternoon teas at the offices of the *Idler* where he met writers, editors, poets, playwrights, and other theatrical figures. He corresponded with Robert Louis Stevenson, though the two never met. James Barrie, who would someday become famous as the author of *Peter Pan,* was a favorite companion; the two shared a love of cricket and an interest in ghosts and fairies.

Throughout the year, ACD churned out more tales of Sherlock Holmes as well as another historical novel, *The Great Shadow.* In November 1892, just four months after the Doyles took an icy cruise to Norway, ACD's second child was born–a son, Alleyne Kingsley. This joy was dampened, however, by an alarming decline in Touie's health. Thinking it would help, ACD arranged a trip to Switzerland, where the Doyles made their way to Reichenbach Falls through severe snowstorms. In the deafening roar of the falls, one could almost imagine hearing shouts and screams. A terrible idea began to take shape in ACD's imagination and, that April, he wrote to his mother, "I am in the middle of the last Holmes story, after which the gentleman vanishes, never to return! I am weary of his name."

Indeed, "death" was the theme of 1893 for ACD. When Touie began to cough up blood, the diagnosis was quickly made—consumption. She had, the doctors said, perhaps only months to live. In October ACD moved the family to Switzerland where he hoped the air would strengthen, if not cure, his beloved wife. Death came then, but not for Touie, who would live another thirteen years. It came instead for ACD's father who died later that month at the mental institution. The Doyles were unable to attend the funeral.

> ✺✺✺✺✺✺✺✺✺✺
>
> **"It has long been an axiom of mine that the little things are infinitely the most important."**
> **—*A Case of Identity***
>
> ✺✺✺✺✺✺✺✺✺✺

"The Adventure of the Final Problem," with its ominous opening words, was published in *The Strand* in December. When Sherlock Holmes fell to his watery death locked in the arms of Professor Moriarty, all of London exploded. Loyal fans were outraged that they had had no warning. Women wept at the news and dressed in mourning clothes, and men donned black silk arm-bands. Over twenty thousand canceled their subscriptions to *The Strand*. Many thousands more wrote angry letters to the publishers. Even the Queen, it is said, was "not amused." Only ACD, steeped in the great mysteries of life and death close to home, seemed oblivious. He would not resurrect Holmes until a year and a half into the new century.

ACD's Great Hiatus

For almost a decade, ACD forgot about Sherlock Holmes, while he filled his life with other things. He revived his latent interest in psychic phenomena and joined the British Society of Psychical Research. He attended numerous séances and investigated haunted houses.

During those years, he socialized with the rich and famous—with the Prime Minister and with Edward VII. He played cricket, golf, billiards, and backgammon, fished with Barrie and lunched with London's literati.

He traveled to Egypt, where he found the Cairo police using Sherlock Holmes adventures as a textbook in detection, and to South Africa, where he volunteered to work with a medical unit during the Boer War. He also traveled with his brother Innes to the U.S., where he maintained a frantic schedule of lectures.

In Boston, toward the end of his tour, he was astonished when a cabby asked to be paid, not in cash, but with an admission ticket to ACD's lecture that evening. When ACD asked how the cabby knew his identity, the driver supposedly answered:

If you will excuse me, your coat lapels are badly twisted downward, where they have been grasped by the pertinacious New York reporters. Your hair has the Quakerish cut of a Philadelphia barber and your hat, battered at the brim in front, shows where you have tightly gasped it, in the struggle to stand your ground at a Chicago literary luncheon. Your right shoe has a large block of Buffalo mud just under the instep; the odor of Utica cigar hangs about your clothing and the overcoat itself shows the slovenly brushing of the porters of the through sleepers from Albany. The crumbs of the doughnut on the top of your waistcoat could only have come there in Springfield.

At ACD's look of total bewilderment, the cabby added with a hearty guffaw, "And stenciled on the very end of your walking stick, in perfectly plain lettering, is the name Conan Doyle!"

In those intervening years before resurrecting Holmes, ACD also fell in love with a woman, not his wife. He told his mother and his closest friends about Jean Leckie, a beautiful young Scottish opera singer. ACD's intellectual and social peer, Leckie would become the great love of his life, though, because he was a Victorian gentleman to the core, ACD was never unfaithful to his wife.

For years, Touie's illness defined ACD's domestic life. In 1897, he moved the family to Hindhead in Surrey in the hope that fresh air would prolong Touie's life. Years later he wrote to his mother, "I tried never to give Touie a moment's unhappiness; to give her every attention, every comfort she could want. Did I succeed? I think so. God knows I hope so."

Through it all, ACD continued to write—horror tales, plays, political tracts, and historical novels. He wrote standing in line for tickets at the railway station or pacing on the platform. He locked himself in his room and wrote through the dinner hour.

One day in 1901, his golf partner at the Royal Links Hotel, Fletcher Robinson, a journalist, told ACD about the legend of a ghostly hound that howls in the wilderness of Dartmoor. It was a tale of a woman accused of infidelity, who was chased onto the moor by her jealous husband and stabbed to death with a hunting knife. After her gruesome end, her devoted hound attacked the knife-wielding man and was himself stabbed to death beside his mistress. To this day, Robinson told ACD, the forlorn howl of the hound could be heard in the ghostly moonlight of the moor.

His imagination piqued, ACD traipsed off to the moor with Robinson to soak up the local lore. The two took rooms in a hotel near the bleak expanse of Dartmoor and toured the area in a trap driven by a man named Baskerville.

The Return of Sherlock Holmes

The first installment of *The Hound of the Baskervilles* appeared in *The Strand* just months later, in August 1901, and ran in seven additional installments through April 1902 to the great delight of the long-suffering readers. By dating the story before the fateful plunge over Reichenbach Falls, it was understood that the master detective was still dead–but postdated tales were better than none at all, and this one was a winner. Reviewers issued raves and with this came publishers' offers of great reward if only Holmes could be truly brought back to life.

ACD relented. Holmes, after all, had refused to die. In the United States,

William Gillette was starring, to great acclaim, in his play, bluntly titled *Sherlock Holmes*. Handsome, eccentric, and reserved, the actor personified the master detective both on stage and off. After hundreds of sold-out performances, the play opened in London's Lyceum Theatre in September 1901, just a month after *Hound* appeared in print. In January 1902, Edward VII caught "Holmes fever," celebrating the end of a year mourning the death of Queen Victoria by taking Queen Alexandra to Gillette's play. Eight months later, a reluctant ACD was knighted, supposedly for a book he wrote on the Boer War and in defense of British conduct.

It seemed there was no denying the reappearance of Sherlock Holmes and so, courted by publishers on both sides of the Atlantic, ACD stuffed large payments in his pockets and once again picked up the pen to breathe new life into his sharp-eyed creation. In 1903, at the age of forty-four, ACD revived Holmes in "The Adventure of the Empty House," first published in the American *Collier's Weekly* and a month later in *The Strand*, and revived his own life with a new hobby–motoring. Decked in cap and goggles, ACD raced along at about fifteen miles an hour in his 12-horsepower Wolseley.

The game was afoot once again for Holmes and Watson, and the publishers couldn't have been happier. Circulation of *The Strand* reached over half a million. Eager readers formed long queues each month on "publication day" to get their copies. Many wrote letters to the detective himself, asking for help solving real-life mysteries. ACD, with the

Jean Leckie, ACD's second wife. They met and fell in love in 1897 and were married in 1907, a year after Touie's death.

help of his secretary, Major Alfred Wood, did his best to reply, though, perhaps as a sign of irritation, sometimes sent postcards without postage, requiring the correspondent to pay upon receipt, and his message was often a blunt statement about Sherlock Holmes–"In the words of Mrs. Gamp, 'there ain't no such person.'" He generally signed the postcards with the name "Dr. John Watson."

ACD was depicted shackled to Sherlock Holmes in this 1926 Punch *caricature drawn by Sir Bernard Partridge.*

Change on the Homefront

In July 1906 ACD's beloved Touie died at the age of 49. This loss, though long anticipated, was devastating for ACD who spent the next months plagued by insomnia and fatigue. What roused him out of his lethargy in December of that year, was a real-life mystery, already three years old, but needing a reversal of judgment and a fair resolution. It was a strange case, with a poison pen as its main weapon and racism at its core.

George Edalji, the accused, came from a quiet, mixed-race family; his mother was Anglo-Saxon; his father, a Parsee Indian, was a minister with the Church of England. The first sign of trouble was an endless stream of threatening letters that were sent to the family, accompanied by graffiti of a similar tone that appeared on the walls of the church and the parish house. Farmers near the parish began to find their animals mutilated. Anonymous letters blamed the polite and studious young George who was, by this time, a lawyer in Birmingham. Though they had very little evidence, the police took the accusatory letters as valid and arrested him. The accused man was convicted and sent to prison for three years, his reputation destroyed.

ACD believed a serious miscarriage of justice had occurred and devoted himself to clearing the man's name and recovering his position as junior barrister. After great effort worthy of his fictional detective, ACD gained the public's sympathy for George Edalji, though not an official reparation, and, more importantly, stirred up enough outrage throughout the nation to justify creation of the Court of Criminal Appeal.

On September 18, 1907, ACD finally married Jean Leckie whose intimate friendship had been maintained throughout the long years of Touie's illness. A honeymoon cruise in the Mediterranean took them to Greece, Egypt, and Turkey where they learned that the Sultan was a great fan of Sherlock Holmes. Back in England for Christmas, ACD once again moved his family, this time to an estate in Sussex called Windlesham. With a billiard room that stretched the entire width of the house and with a garden of rose bowers, this home was truly ACD's castle.

In the next five years, ACD and Jean had two sons and a daughter. The growth of his family did nothing to deter the author from his work. He was an obsessive writer, maintaining a schedule that began at 6:30 every morning, and he still wrote on the go, even while waiting in traffic. He wrote about everything, from reform in the Congo to ghosts in the attic. He also continued to write plays, which he sometimes financed and directed himself. In his dramatization, "The Speckled Band," he insisted that a real snake play the title role. The rock boa, however, got less than rave reviews when it refused to slither, or, indeed, move.

In 1911 ACD wrote a science fiction novel, *The Lost World,* in which Professor Challenger and his journalist sidekick Edward Malone discover dinosaurs in modern-day South America. The book became a bestseller and was quickly followed the next year by another Challenger story, *The Poison Belt.*

Throughout his life, ACD was tireless in public debate about a range of issues: he opposed women's suffrage, the use of feathers in ladies' hats, and home rule for Ireland (a position he later reversed); he supported divorce law reform, oral teaching of the deaf, and the construction of a tunnel across the English Channel. He wrote pamphlets in defense of the Crown and lost two campaigns for a seat in Parliament as a Unionist candidate.

Public controversy didn't faze him. In 1912 ACD engaged in a war of words with Bernard Shaw about the crew of the *Titanic*. Over 1,500 of the 2,200 aboard had drowned when the British liner sank after hitting an iceberg on her maiden voyage. Whereas others lauded the dead sailors as heroes and told romantic stories of the disaster, Shaw denounced the crew as inefficient and unprepared and accused Captain Smith of incompetence. He called the lack of lifeboats a national scandal and noted with scorn the failure of the crew to assist the steerage passengers. ACD was outraged at Shaw's accusations aimed at seamen who could not vindicate themselves. He defended Captain Smith as an "old and honored sailor who has made one terrible mistake, and who deliberately gave his life in reparation."

For some time, ACD had had premonitions about German aggression. In 1911 he participated in the Prince Henry Automobile Race, which pitted fifty German cars against fifty cars driven by members of the Royal Automobile Club. It was intended to be a good-will event for the two countries, but ACD developed the uneasy feeling that the Germans were deliberately distracting the British with games. Something wasn't right. Two weeks after ACD and his family returned from an American/Canadian tour, World War I erupted. ACD formed a local volunteer corps, practiced formation marching, and did fund-raising for the war effort. In the midst of the war, ACD penned his Sherlock Holmes novella *The Valley of Fear,* and, in the story, "His Last Bow," involved Holmes in the capture of a German spy.

> "It is an old maxim of mine that when you have excluded the impossible, whatever remains, however improbable, must be the truth."
> —*The Adventure of the Beryl Coronet*

Spirits, Fairies, and the Psychic Question

The war marked a major turning point for ACD. His lifelong curiosity about spiritualism and sympathetic but capricious interest in séances and haunted houses took a serious turn. Against the background of a world war, ACD became a believer and, for the rest of his life, spiritualism was his consuming passion. In his public declaration, *The New Revelation,* ACD explained the impact of the war on his thinking:

> In the presence of an agonized world, hearing every day of the deaths of the flower of our race in the first promise of their unfulfilled youth, seeing around one the wives and mothers who had no clear conception whither their loved one had gone to, I seemed

Throughout his life, ACD participated in séances, much like the one depicted here.
Credit: Bettmann Archive, New York.

suddenly to see that this subject with which I had so long dallied was not merely a study of a force outside the rules of science, but that it was really something tremendous, a breaking down of the walls between two worlds, a direct undeniable message from beyond, a call of hope and of guidance to the human race at the time of its deepest affliction.

For ACD, as for others who survived the horrors of World War I, spiritualism offered consolation to grieving families and friends, bewildered that the mass slaughter had so intimately touched their lives. For spiritualists, the dead were gone–but not far. Mothers saw their dead sons solemnly standing guard near the family home. "Spirit photographs" taken in cemeteries showed

ghostly faces hovering over grave sites. Soldiers saw their dead friends wandering between the troops on the battlefields. One boy reportedly came back from the grave, pointed an ethereal finger at the floor boards of a dugout and successfully warned his buddies about a land mine buried there.

By 1917 ACD was immersed in reading and lecturing on spiritualism, which he now approached, "not in the spirit of a detective approaching a suspect, but in that of a humble religious soul, yearning for help and comfort." He would need the help and comfort of his new faith. His wife's brother was killed in the war, then other friends and relatives. In October 1918 ACD was about to deliver a talk when he was handed a telegram that his wounded soldier-son, Kingsley, was dying of influenza. ACD paused, just briefly, to register his shock and grief, and then went on to present his speech. In February 1919 his beloved younger brother Innes also died of pneumonia while recovering from a war wound.

These might have been devastating losses had it not been for ACD's conviction that the soul is immortal and sentient and that the living could establish communications with the spirits of the dead. According to one biographer, within hours after hearing of Kingsley's death, ACD contacted him via a medium and was reassured that his son was courageously finding his way through the mists of death. Throughout the rest of his life, ACD stayed in regular contact with both Kingsley and Innes through various mediums.

His new religion became the driving force of ACD's life. It was not enough that he had been converted to spiritualism; he wanted the world to understand its relevance. In "The Psychic Question as I See It" he wrote:

> I consider [spiritualism] to be infinitely the most important thing in the world, and the particular thing which the human race in its present state of development needs more than anything else.

ACD lectured throughout Europe, Australia, Africa, and North America, visiting both Canada and the U.S., and wrote thirteen books and numerous articles advocating spiritualism and defending its proponents from charges of fraud. As the most famous convert to spiritualism, his lecture tours drew large crowds of both the faithful and the skeptical, and sometimes had unexpect-

ed results. After a series of lectures in New York City, there was a frenzy of suicides and a few mercy killings by those for whom the promise of the "Great Beyond" was irresistible.

In 1920 ACD met Harry Houdini. Famous for his ability to escape from seemingly impossible situations, Houdini was also known for his commitment to exposing fake mediums. His was a love/hate affair with spiritualism, a belief system to which he was instinctively drawn, but toward which he maintained a stoic cynicism. Despite their differences, ACD and Houdini became close friends for a time.

During a trip to the States in 1922 Jean Doyle, who had herself become a medium adept at automatic writing, invited Houdini to a private séance. She offered to open a channel of communication with Houdini's beloved mother. He accepted the invitation, hoping against hope that contact could be made, and watched in anguish as Lady Doyle's pen was driven with remarkable speed across sheets of paper in an unrestrained message of love. Unfortunately the missive was in perfect English, a language Houdini's mother did not know. Houdini waited until the Doyles departed from America before going public with a derisive account of the séance. The friendship never recovered.

A new controversy presented itself in the summer of 1920 with the report that two young girls in Yorkshire had proven the existence of fairies by photographing them. ACD examined the photographs which showed miniscule female figures sporting delicate, transparent wings. He was convinced. In his book *The Coming of the Fairies* ACD wrote:

Other well-authenticated cases will come along. These little folk who appear to be our neighbors, with only some small differences of vibration to separate us, will become familiar. The thought of them, even when unseen, will add a charm to every brook and valley.

This latest crusade, to prove the existence of fairies, inspired even more ridicule and scorn than ACD's conversion to spiritualism or his fascination with "spirit photographs." The press had a field day, and the London *Star* published a photograph of ACD with fairies dancing around his head. How could this staunch no-nonsense Victorian patriarch, whose feet were so firmly planted on the cricket field, defend such fantasies?

Could this be the same man who had established worldwide fame by creating the detective affectionately described as a "reasoning and observing machine"? Indeed, Sherlock Holmes, unlike his author, continued to dismiss all talk of ghosts as lunacy and to express his skepticism about the supernatural with unrepentant amusement. He "placed true cold reason" above all things.

Fans of the master detective were perplexed at best and occasionally ACD's lectures were interrupted by hecklers who called him the "Anti-Christ." The accusations and ridicule had little effect on ACD, nor was his faith undermined by personal experience with fraudulent mediums, such as the spirit control at one séance who insisted on addressing ACD as "Sir Sherlock Holmes." ACD simply disre-

garded those he regarded as fakes. Spirit contact with the Ma'am, who had died at age eighty-three while the Doyles were on a trip to Australia, and messages from his brother and his son, continued to sustain ACD's faith.

The End of Holmes

Throughout the last decade of his life, ACD maintained the attention to order that had always characterized his daily regime, neatly balancing family, work, and play. In 1924 and '25 he wrote a series of Sherlock Holmes stories, including one published in a miniature book called "How Watson Learned the Trick" for the tiny library of the Queen's Doll House. After writing "The Adventure of Shoscombe Old Place," ACD announced Holmes's retirement. This time, there was no public outcry.

ACD set up a second home, Bignell House, in Hampshire where he could hold séances without constant interruption. His new neighbors, however, were suspicious and hostile. The mail carrier refused to deliver letters to the house and a priest in a nearby village exorcised evil entities that the locals claimed had emanated from ACD's house.

Despite the constant tension he provoked in unbelievers, ACD carried on, sustained by crowds of admirers. At the Armistice Day spiritualist meeting in 1926, thousands attended, and, when ACD cried out for all those who were in touch with their dead to rise and testify, three thousand stood in silent witness. A speaking tour to Africa in 1928 and to Scandinavia and Holland in 1929 made new converts and reinforced ACD's own belief in spiritualism. His faith even sustained him through the isolation that resulted when he resigned from the Society of Psychical Research, believing it had become hostile to authentic inquiry.

After-Life Activities

After a period of seclusion in his Sussex home, Windlesham ACD died at age seventy-one, on July 7, 1930, and was buried on the grounds of the estate. On his grave marker were inscribed the words "Steel True, Blade Straight."

Death barely put a dent in ACD's social schedule. Within twenty-four hours, various family members had received messages from the "other side." The eight thousand people who attended ACD's funeral were told by a medium that he was present in his evening clothes. She described for the mourners his approach to an empty chair, and part of his message to Lady Doyle.

Three days after his death he appeared to fifteen people gathered at a séance in the Bronx and told them, "I want to write a book while I'm here." Later he conveyed a message via a clairvoyant to a group in Vancouver, reassuring them that he had received warm welcomes from the "spirit folk."

Jean Doyle, who was able to transcribe the messages from her husband with automatic writing, announced to the press at the end of July that ACD had most definitely established communication through a spirit photograph. In February of the following year, Lady Doyle and the Doyle's youngest son Adrian attended a séance at which ACD's voice was projected from the mouth of a flying trumpet. For more than an hour, ACD discussed family affairs with them.

These messages from "the beyond" continued for years. In 1936, the dead ACD, still conversant in medical matters, diagnosed Jean's cancer. Until her death in 1940, Lady Doyle appreciated ACD's ongoing advice about the family business investments, warnings of impending danger, and messages of affection.

P U Z Z L E R

Colors in the Canon

—•~•~•—

Complete these titles by finding the corresponding colors.

1. A Study in _____.   A. COPPER

2. The Adventure of the _____ Circle.   B. YELLOW

3. The Five _____ Pips.   C. SCARLET

4. The Adventure of the _____ Carbuncle.   D. GOLDEN

5. The Adventure of the _____ Beeches.   E. RED

6. The Adventure of _____ Blaze.   F. BLUE

7. The Adventure of the _____ Face.   G. BLACK

8. The Adventure of _____ Peter.   H. ORANGE

9. The Adventure of the _____ Pince-Nez.   I. SILVER

Solutions: 1-C; 2-E; 3-H; 4-F; 5-A; 6-I; 7-B; 8-G; 9-D

CAPSULE

A Case of Identity

First Publication:

The Strand Magazine, September 1891

Principal Predicament:

Mary Sutherland, a large, lonely woman with a vacuous face, has been duti-fully handing over her monthly inheritance to her stepfather. In a rare moment of independence, albeit when her stepfather was out of town, she went to the Gasfitters' Ball and met Mr. Hosmer Angel. They continued to see each other on the sly when the stepfather was away and planned to marry, but the groom mysteriously disappeared on his way to the church. He hasn't been heard from since. Holmes advises her to forget Mr. Angel, but the broken-hearted woman says she intends to remain true.

Notable Feature:

This is generally considered to be a disappointing story on several counts. First, it presents a woman so naive and unobservant that the story is unbeliev-able. Second, Holmes is powerless to help the pathetic victim or punish the culprit.

Quotable Quote:

Holmes: *"Life is infinitely stranger than anything which the mind of man could invent."*

Miss Mary Sutherland had hoped to eat her wedding breakfast at the St. Pancras Hotel.

CAPSULE

The Boscombe Valley Mystery

First Publication:

The Strand Magazine, October 1891

Principal Predicament:

Ex-Australian Charles McCarthy was seen arguing violently with his son out by the old Boscombe Pool. Moments later, his lovesick son James appeared at a nearby lodge to say that he had found his father dead in the wood. James has, of course, been locked up and charged with "wilful murder." The facts seem obvious, but, after inspecting the area around Boscombe Pool with a lens, Holmes concludes that the murderer is a tall, left-handed man who limps with the right leg, wears thick-soled shooting boots and a gray cloak, smokes Indian cigars, uses a cigar holder, and carries a blunt pen knife in his pocket.

Notable Feature:

Holmes is described as wearing "a long gray travelling cloak and close-fitting cloth cap." This inspired illustrator Sidney Paget to draw the famed cloak and deerstalker outfit that has become an enduring image of the master detective.

Quotable Quote:

Holmes: *"Many men have been wrongfully hanged."*

Oddities and Discrepancies

At the end of the story Holmes contemplates the tricks of fate and laments, "I never hear of such a case as this that I do not think of Baxter's words, and say, 'There, but for the grace of God, goes Sherlock Holmes.'" But who is Baxter? Holmes's paraphrase is of a famous saying by John Bradford.

The Five Orange Pips

First Publication:

The Strand Magazine, November 1891

Principal Predicament:

A family curse seems to be plaguing poor John Openshaw. He has received an envelope marked with "K.K.K." containing five dried orange seeds. There's also a demand, "Put the papers on the sundial." When his Uncle Elias received a similar sign in March 1883 he was found, seven weeks later, dead in a pool of green-scummed water. In January 1885 his father, Joseph Openshaw, had shattered his skull in a fall over a chalk pit just three days after receiving an envelope marked "K.K.K.," also containing five orange pips. Somehow, it all seems connected to the years Uncle Elias spent in America, where he had made a small fortune. Elias had left the States because of his "aversion to the negroes" and his opposition to giving them the right to vote. What does all this have to do with fruit seeds?

The Ku Klux Klan, a secret terrorist organization, was started in 1866 in Tennessee. Credit: Bettmann Archive, New York.

Notable Features:

This is one of Sherlock Holmes's failures, though it is hardly his fault. And, unlike most of the stories in the Canon, this one does not stand the test of time. Readers in 1891 might have been mystified by the clues and, with Watson, could ask, "Who is this K.K.K. and why does he pursue this unhappy family?" Sadly, the initials hold no mystery at all for readers in the late twentieth century, but immediately bring to mind images of white-sheeted terrorists.

Quotable Quotes:

Holmes: *"I am the last court of appeal."*
Holmes: *"I have been beaten four times–three times by men, and once by a woman."*

The Man with the Twisted Lip

First Publication:

The Strand Magazine, December 1891

Principal Predicament:

Mrs. St. Clair went to town on Monday to do some shopping. In the late afternoon she found herself in a disagreeable part of the city where, hearing a cry, she was struck cold to see her husband, Neville, frantically waving his hands at her from a second-floor window of the flat over an opium den. Accompanied by two constables and an inspector, she rushed up to the room, only to find Hugh Boone, an orange-haired, crippled beggar with a twisted lip. There was no sign of her husband, only his clothing and a box of children's bricks. One window of the apartment looked out over the wharf and the river. When blood is found on the windowsill, even Holmes concludes that poor Neville is dead in the water. But on Friday, Mrs. St. Clair receives a letter from her husband.

Notable Feature:

Holmes shows himself a master of disguise, as he sits in an opium den, an old man, very wrinkled and bent with age. Nevertheless, by story's end, he says, "I think, Watson, that you are now standing in the presence of one of the most absolute fools in Europe. I deserve to be kicked from here to Charing Cross."

Quotable Quote:

Holmes: *"You have a grand gift of silence, Watson. It makes you quite invaluable as a companion."*

Oddities and Discrepancies:

Is Mrs. Watson confused? We know Dr. Watson as John, but his wife, perhaps weary of her needlework and ready for bed, inexplicably refers to him as "James."

Holmes's London

———

London at the time of the Sherlock Holmes series was a city that was in many ways the first of its kind. Teeming with numbers unimaginable before the industrial and transportation revolutions, London could be described either as "that great cesspool" as Watson opines at the opening of the Canon, or as Dr. Samuel Johnson did a century before, "When a man is tired of London he is tired of life, for there is in London all that life may afford."

London had been a city of importance in England since Roman times, though it had declined at various periods, particularly after the Roman retreat from the island in the fifth century A.D. Its population was estimated at 40,000 in 1199, just over a century after the Norman invasion, making it a respectable urban area by contemporary European standards.

By the late seventeenth century it had risen to the neighborhood of half a million. In 1801, the first reasonably reliable census, there were 1.1 million, a figure that was to be multiplied by a factor of five a century later.

As Roy Porter wrote in *London, a Social History,* the city's population in Holmes's time "far exceeded Switzerland and Australia–it had twice the numbers of Norway or Greece. In London there were more Scotsmen than in Aberdeen, more Irishmen than in Dublin, and more Roman Catholics than in Rome."

Post-Dickensian Reality

The picture of London in the nineteenth century that emerges from Dickens and other contemporary writers is often dominated by images of poverty and squalor, the workhouse and the rookery. While there was much truth to their portraits, the other side of Victorian and London life was the growth of the lower middle and working classes, to better housing and health, education, longer lives, and even leisure.

The characters in the Holmes stories, many of whom lived in the London area, range from the street urchins of the Baker Street Irregulars to the solid

The railroad permitted European cities to grow to enormous size, particularly London, which by the turn of the twentieth century held more than five million people.

middle class of the suburban builder, the landed and industrial aristocracy, and even foreign royalty.

As the most urbanized, productive, and prosperous area in the most urbanized, productive, and prosperous nation in the world, London was a center of industry, trade, finance, and culture.

It held one in five residents of the nation, its national government and bank, its leading cultural institutions. The Port of London in Holmes's time accepted more than 8 million tons of shipping per year (and exported some 6 million). While there were manufacturing operations elsewhere, particularly in the north of England, London remained

a center for activities as various as shipbuilding, publishing, matchmaking, silk weaving, and pottery and furniture making.

East vs. West

In terms of social geography, the operative distinction in London was between the East End and the West.

The East End was the home of the Thames docks and the working and poorer classes in Stepney and Limehouse where, as Watson notes in *A Study in Scarlet,* "the tenement houses swelter and reek with the outcasts of Europe."

The upper and middle classes occu-

A hansom cab on Baker Street, 1900. Credit: From the collection of William Gordon Davis

pied the West End bastions of Belgravia, Mayfair, Kensington, Regent's Park, and other areas in which we may presume the occupants rarely sweltered and if so never reeked.

These districts were in general east and west of a line drawn north from the City, the original area of London north of the Thames, which by the late nineteenth century had become an office district.

In "The Man with the Twisted Lip,"

Mrs. Neville St. Clair lives in the southeastern suburb of Lee, but finds herself in the area east of the City near her train station at Cannon Street "glancing about in the hope of seeing a cab, as she did not like the neighborhood in which she found herself." The "sinister cripple" Hugh Boone, a professional beggar, lived nearby above an opium den on Swandam Lane when not plying his trade nearby on Threadneedle Street.

London's Hyde Park.

On the other side of the City lay the West End. It included the City of Westminster, site of the royal palaces and government offices, and retreats of the titled, the important or the merely well-off. It is on Serpentine Avenue in the West End neighborhood of St. John's Wood that Holmes goes to recover an offending photograph from the chanteuse Irene Adler and to Hampstead to deal with the society blackmailer Charles Augustus Milverton.

Baker Street itself lies in the West End, tolerably close to Hyde Park, Park Lane, Regent Street, and intersecting with Oxford Street. Holmes was close to the centers of power and influence (Whitehall, where brother Mycroft was a key government functionary, and to Kensington Palace, where he was occasionally useful).

Growing Outward Rather Than Up

Yet the adventures of Sherlock Holmes took him and Watson into virtually every corner of the expanding city.

While New York was growing upward at this time, thanks to the limited availability of land and the invention of the elevator, London, like Chicago, had room to grow on its outskirts, particularly as horse-drawn omnibuses and trams, and the construction of ever more bridges across the Thames let it explode outward to the north, the west, and most particularly the south.

In *The Sign of the Four* Holmes and Watson are driven over the Vauxhall Bridge to one of the new neighborhoods created south of the Thames by the city's growth, "rows of two-storied villas, each with a fronting of miniature garden, and then again interminable lines of new, staring brick buildings—the monster tentacles which the giant city was throwing out into the country."

"It is a hobby of mine to have an exact knowledge of London," Holmes told Watson, but the great detective knew it could be no more than a hobby, so rapidly was the city changing. For London, like other places becoming world cities in the last half of the nineteenth century, was changing at a phenomenal rate. But for the occasional landmark saved by accident or design, lifelong residents of London (or New York for that matter) had the experience of losing the city of their youth.

It was not because they had moved—it was because the city had moved beyond them, neighborhoods changing almost overnight, new construction revising its physical shape, residents moving on to other areas, immigration reshaping the linguistic and cultural landscape.

> **"It is of the highest importance in the art of detection to be able to recognize, out of a number of facts, which are incidental and which vital. Otherwise your energy and attention must be dissipated instead of being concentrated."**
> —*The Adventure of the Reigate Squires*

The Sherlock Holmes Mystery Map of London

1. BAKER STREET. Holmes and Watson shared rooms at 221. The "B" indicates that the duo's rooms were on an upper floor. Mrs. Hudson lived on the ground floor.
2. PADDINGTON STATION. Holmes and Watson caught the train for the Boscombe Valley here and Sir Henry Baskerville left for the haunted Dartmoor.
3. HYDE PARK. Holmes and Watson strolled here in comfortable silence in "The Yellow Face."
4. PALL MALL. Holmes's older brother Mycroft was a founding member of the Diogenes Club, located here.
5. BROAD STREET. Opening onto the Thames, Mordecai Smith's landing stage for his steam launch, *Aurora,* was here in *The Sign of the Four.*
6. DOWNING STREET. Holmes met with Lord Holdhurst here in the Foreign Office regarding the missing naval treaty.
7. NEW SCOTLAND YARD. Headquarters of the Metropolitan Police, Holmes kept in touch with all that was going on there.
8. VICTORIA STATION. In "Final Problem," Holmes and Watson got a train here, barely escaping Moriarty.
9. REGENT STREET. Holmes was attacked here by Baron Gruner's gang of thugs outside the Café Royal in "The Illustrious Client."
10. GOODGE STREET. Henry Baker lost his hat and his Christmas goose when he was challenged by street roughs in "Blue Carbuncle."
11. ST. JAMES'S HALL. Holmes and Watson interrupted their investigation of the Red-Headed League to attend a concert here.
12. CHARING CROSS STATION. In "Illustrious Client," Watson stood stunned when he saw the one-legged newsvender's placard proclaiming "Murderous Attack upon Sherlock Holmes."
13. MONTAGUE STREET. Before moving to Baker Street, Holmes had rooms here.
14. FLEET STREET. In "Resident Patient," Holmes and Watson strolled along this busy thoroughfare, watching the kaleidoscope of London life. The offices of the Red-Headed League were located near here.
15. ST. BARTHOLOMEW'S HOSPITAL. Where young Stamford first introduced Holmes and Watson.
16. COVENT GARDEN THEATRE. In "Red Circle," Holmes and Watson attended a Wagner performance here.
17. NORTHUMBERLAND AVENUE. Where Holmes and Watson lay side by side at their favorite Turkish bath.

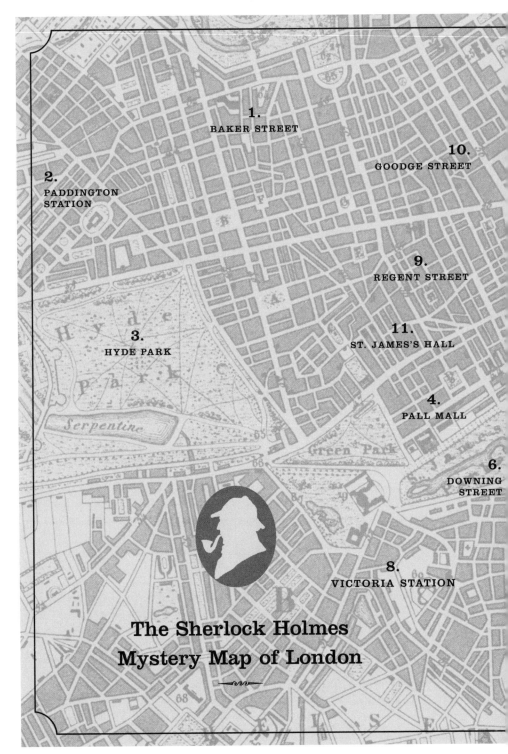

1.
BAKER STREET

10.
GOODGE STREET

2.
PADDINGTON
STATION

9.
REGENT STREET

3.
HYDE PARK

11.
ST. JAMES'S HALL

4.
PALL MALL

6.
DOWNING
STREET

8.
VICTORIA STATION

Serpentine

The Sherlock Holmes
Mystery Map of London

13.
MONTAGUE
STREET

16.
COVENT GARDEN
THEATRE

15.
ST. BARTHOLOMEW'S
HOSPITAL

14.
FLEET STREET

12.
CHARING CROSS
STATION

River Thames

17.
NORTHUMBERLAND
AVENUE

7.
NEW
SCOTLAND
YARD

5.
BROAD
STREET

The Adventure of the Blue Carbuncle

First Publication:

The Strand Magazine, January 1892

Principal Predicament:

On the second morning after Christmas, Watson arrives at Baker Street to find Holmes in a purple dressing gown, studying a very seedy hat. Early on Christmas morning, Peterson, a commissionaire, was headed home when he encountered some roughs harassing a tall man carrying a Christmas goose. One of the naughty boys knocked the man's hat off and the man, waving his cane in self-defense, accidently broke a store window. Peterson rushed to protect the victim who misunderstood the commissionaire's intent and apparently feared repercussions for the window he'd broken. Both the man and his attackers fled from the well-intentioned Peterson, leaving behind, not only a hat, but the goose. Holmes has barely finished demonstrating to Watson just how much one can deduce about a person from a hat, when Peterson bursts into the apartment gasping, "The goose, Mr. Holmes! The goose, sir!" It seems he's found a remarkable blue gem inside the Christmas goose. Holmes knows right way that it is *the* blue carbuncle belonging to the Countess of Morcar. But how did it get inside the goose and who put it there?

Notable Feature:

This is the only mystery set during the Christmas season. It is also a rare case in which Holmes believes he might be instrumental in "saving a soul," saying in his own defense, "it is the season of forgiveness."

Oddities and Discrepancies

The carbuncle, a precious stone, comes in many colors–white, yellow, red, purple, green–but not blue.

CAPSULE

The Adventure of the Speckled Band

First Publication:

The Strand Magazine, February 1892

Principal Predicament:

Helen Stoner arrives early one morning at Baker Street in a very agitated state. She reports that, as she lay in bed the night before, she heard a low whistle. The last time she heard that sound was two years ago, just moments before the tortured death of her twin sister. Helen tells her mysterious story and leaves. Before Holmes and Watson can digest what they've just heard, Helen's huge, angry stepfather, Dr. Grimesby Roylott, barges into the room taunting Holmes with names and threats, and bends a fireplace poker with his bare hands.

"Where does that bell communicate with?" he asked at last, pointing to a thick bell-rope which hung down beside the bed, the tassel actually lying upon the pillow. Credit: Ana Capitaine, illustrator.

Notable Feature:

This story was Conan Doyle's favorite and, since its publication, has generally been considered a favorite by readers as well.

Quotable Quote:

Holmes: *"When a doctor does go wrong he is the first of criminals. He has nerve and he has knowledge."*

Oddities and Discrepancies:

What was Julia Stoner doing with her hands when she died? She's described as groping for help, pointing her finger in stabbing movements, and, while groping and pointing, also clutching the stump of a match in her right hand and match box in her left.

The Adventure of the Engineer's Thumb

First Publication:

The Strand Magazine, March 1892

Principal Predicament:

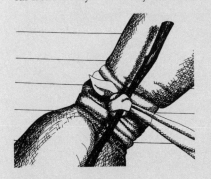

Mr. Victor Hatherley, a hydraulic engineer, arrives at Dr. Watson's office pale, on the verge of hysteria, and missing a thumb. According to his account, he had been engaged by Colonel Stark to repair a broken hydraulic press not far from the Eyford railway station, and was sworn to absolute secrecy from the start. He was met at the railway station, taken via a meandering route to his destination, and rushed into a pitch-dark house. Shortly after his arrival, a woman urgently warns him to "get away from here before it is too late!" Hatherley, however, stays long enough to discover, not only what is wrong with the hydraulic press, but its real function. With that knowledge, he barely escapes with his life.

Notable Features:

This is a rare case brought to Holmes by Watson. There is, however, no mystery to unravel. Holmes is called upon only to help apprehend the villains. At the end of the story, Holmes consoles the victim by suggesting that he will benefit by having an interesting story to tell for the rest of his life.

Oddities and Discrepancies

Hatherley had a hat when he arrived at Watson's office. But, assuming that he was not wearing it as he worked on the broken press and that he did not have time to grab it as he was escaping, how was it that he was so completely attired when he arrived for medical attention? And, considering the angle of the weapon in relation to the position of Hatherley's hands, it is difficult to come up with a reasonable explanation of just how his thumb was severed, or, even, which thumb it was.

The Adventure of the Noble Bachelor

First Publication:

The Strand Magazine, April 1892

Principal Predicament:

Lord Robert St. Simon, a gentleman whose dress verges on foppishness and whose mouth displays a touch of petulance, has married the beautiful Hatty Doran. In her youth, the bride had been a high-spirited tomboy running free in an American mining camp, before her father struck gold and became the richest man on the Pacific slope. The wedding was a quiet one, marred only by the odd moment, after the exchange of vows, when the bride dropped her bouquet into the front pew. A gentleman quickly retrieved it and handed it back to her. A short time later, the new wife of Lord Robert St. Simon utterly vanished. The groom is sure that anything dishonorable would be repugnant to his new wife, but fears she may have become deranged under the pressure of making an immense social stride. The police, however, fear foul play. They are especially concerned that the groom's old flame, the broken-hearted, hot-headed Flora Miller, may have decoyed Hatty and laid some terrible trap for her. They are dragging the lake in Hyde Park, looking for Hatty's body. Hearing this, Holmes blows blue smoke rings into the air.

Notable Feature:

Conan Doyle, in a letter to a friend, ranked this story "about the bottom of the list."

Oddities and Discrepancies

Watson and Holmes both call the jilted groom Lord St. Simon. As the second son of the Duke of Balmoral, he would be called Lord Robert St. Simon or simply Lord Robert.

Detectives Official and Un. . . .

Arthur Conan Doyle owed an obvious debt of gratitude to the writers who preceded him in the detective genre–Edgar Allan Poe ("The Gold Bug"), Émile Gaboriau (*LeCoq the detective*) and Wilkie Collins (*The Moonstone*).

But when Sherlock Holmes applies his famous logic to individuals and situations, he does so in honor and imitation not of a detective, but of an otherwise obscure Scottish physician and university lecturer, Dr. Joseph Bell.

Bell was an instructor at Edinburgh University, where Conan Doyle took a medical degree. He was renowned there for his ability to detect symptoms and even diagnose maladies with minimal information, sometimes without even talking to the patients.

In his autobiography, Conan Doyle speaks of his admiration for previous detective story writes and characters, but wonders "Could I bring an addition of my own? I thought of my old teacher Joe Bell, of his eagle face, of his curious ways, of his eerie trick of spotting details. If he were a detective he would surely reduce this fascinating business to something nearer an exact science."

It was no accident that it was a physician who practiced and taught such a procedure. Virtually the only diagnostic instruments physicians possessed were stethoscopes and their own eyes and other senses. In an era before the wide use of X rays and blood tests, decades before things like sonograms and CAT scans were even contemplated, careful observation of patients' manner, walk, skin color, clarity of eye were most of what a doctor had to go on in diagnosing the presence and cause of ailments.

> "It is a curious thing, that a typewriter has really quite as much individuality as a man's handwriting. Unless they are quite new, no two of them write exactly alike."
> —*A Case of Identity*

Dr. Joseph Bell of Edinburgh University, an inspiration for Sherlock Holmes.

The Marks of a Craft

Bell was famous for his ability to distinguish the marks of individual professions and crafts on the hands and bodies of patients, and it is this talent, greatly extended, that Holmes so often demonstrates.

"By a man's fingernails, by his coat-sleeve, by his boots, by his trouser-knees, by the callosities of his forefinger and thumb, by his expression, by his shirtsleeve–by each of these things a man's calling is plainly revealed," he tells Watson in *A Study in Scarlet.*

Holmes's powers of observation play a role in virtually every story, but one of the earliest examples of the method comes in "The Red-Headed League," as Holmes looks at his potential client, Mr. Jabez Wilson, and remarks, "beyond the obvious facts that he has at some time done manual labor, that he takes snuff,

that he is a Freemason, that he has been in China, and that he has done a considerable amount of writing lately, I can deduce nothing else."

The skill reaches perhaps its highest expression in "The Adventure of the Greek Interpreter," as Holmes and his brother Mycroft stare out the window of a London club at a man neither knows. In an inquiring if somewhat competitive spirit they determine him to be, in order, an old soldier, recently discharged, a veteran of India, a noncommissioned officer, probably of the artillery, and a recent widower with young children.

At Watson's insistence that "this is a little too much," Sherlock replies, "it is not hard to say that a man with that bearing, expression of authority, and sun-baked skin, is a soldier, more than a private, and not long from India."

Adds Mycroft, "That he has not left the service long is shown by his still wearing his ammunition boots, as they are called."

"He had not the cavalry stride, yet he wore his hat on one side, as is shown by the lighter skin on that side of his brow. His weight is against his being a sapper. He is in the artillery."

"Then of course his complete mourning shows that he has lost someone very dear. The fact that he is doing shopping looks as though it were his wife. He has been buying things for children, you perceive. There is a rattle which shows that one of them is very young. The wife probably died in childbed. The fact that he has a picture-book under his arm shows that there is another child to be thought of."

Yet it is Watson who typically offers the descriptions that make us aware of

The Metropolitan Police moved to New Scotland Yard in 1890. Holmes liked to keep in touch with all that was going on there.

the inner life and character, rather than the occupation, of the person described. Mycroft Holmes's "light, watery gray" eyes, for instance, "seemed always to retain that far-away introspective look which I had only observed in Sherlock's face when he was exerting his full powers."

He describes "the craggy and deeply seamed face with the fierce eyes and hawklike nose" of the African explorer Dr. Sterndale in "The Adventure of the Devil's Foot"; the "lovely mask-like face with two wonderful Spanish eyes which looked murder at us both" of the adventuress Isadora Klein in "The Adventure of the Three Gables"; and the utterly illuminating portrait of Lord Robert St. Simon, of "The Adventure of the Noble

Bachelor," "a pleasant, cultured face, high-nosed and pale, with something perhaps of petulance about the mouth, and with the steady, well-opened eye of a man whose pleasant lot it had ever been to command and to be obeyed."

Detection, Deduction, and the "Official" Police

Strictly speaking, Holmes's usual chain of reasoning, from the particular to the general, is properly described as induction, not deduction. Holmes detects details other observers miss, and draws inferences from them.

"It is of the highest importance in the art of detection to be able to recognize, out of a number of facts, which are incidental and which vital," he told Watson in "The Adventure of the Reigate Squires."

That such an ability seemed out of reach of the "official" police was a source of patronizing amusement to Holmes.

Scotland Yard, as the official police were and are known, covered both uniformed officers and detectives (the Criminal Investigation Division). Founded in 1829, its first headquarters was near the site of a castle that had been used for centuries by Scottish kings when they visited London. Although the headquarters has been relocated, the name has survived.

Scotland Yard's jurisdiction in Holmes's time included only London and its environs (though not "the City" or financial district, which had its own force). Crimes outside the metropolitan district were therefore the responsibility of regional police forces. However, Scotland Yard could be called in on particularly difficult or significant cases.

The overwhelming majority of stories include some involvement of Scotland Yard or local police agencies. Holmes seemed to blow hot and cold on Inspector Lestrade, who figures in more than a dozen stories, finding him "lacking in imagination" but possessing "bull-

---

"Never trust to general impressions, my boy, but concentrate yourself upon details. My first glance is always at a woman's sleeve. In a man it is perhaps better first to take the knee of the trouser."
—*A Case of Identity*

---

dog tenacity." Inspector Tobias Gregson, who is mentioned in four stories, and Inspector Bradstreet, mentioned in three, fare little better.

Still, in "The Adventure of the Three Garridebs," Holmes concedes that the Yard "leads the world in thoroughness and method" and Holmes was prepared to tolerate and even encourage members of the Yard when they showed promise, particularly by recognizing his genius for what it was.

"We're not jealous of you at Scotland Yard. No, sir, we are very proud of you," Inspector Lestrade tells Holmes, with perhaps a bit of exaggeration, in "The Adventure of the Six Napoleons."

But perhaps the ultimate acknowledgment of the Holmesian method comes from Inspector Macdonald, whose "keen intelligence" Watson notes in *The Valley of Fear*. Holmes is discussing with Macdonald the reality behind the respectable facade of Professor Moriarty, whose rooms Macdonald had visited.

"Did you happen to observe a picture over the professor's head?" Holmes asks.

"I don't miss much, Mr. Holmes," Macdonald replies. "Maybe I learned that from you."

Basil Rathbone as Sherlock Holmes. Courtesy Foto Fantasies.

The Role of a Lifetime

⟨⟨ivi⟩⟩

Dozens, perhaps hundreds of actors have portrayed Sherlock Holmes on stage, in film, radio, and television. Many, like Eille Norwood and Arthur Wontner, while famous in their time, are now footnotes to theatrical history. Others, like John Barrymore, Michael Caine, George C. Scott, and Nicol Williamson, earned their fame in other roles.

But three men virtually defined the dramatic Holmes during their own periods: William Gillette, Basil Rathbone, and Jeremy Brett. They *became* Holmes, sometimes to their regret, to a vast audience.

A Connecticut Yankee

The first legitimate Holmes stage production began with Conan Doyle himself, who sent a Holmes drama to a London impresario in the late 1890s. It was passed on to an American producer, and through him to a famous American actor, William Gillette.

Gillette, a U.S. Senator's son from

William Gillette as Holmes. Courtesy Museum of Modern Art/Film Stills Archive.

Hartford, Connecticut, who had been successful as an actor and playwright since 1875, asked permission to rewrite the play along his own lines.

Conan Doyle agreed, and in 1899 Gillette sailed to England to show Conan Doyle the new version. According to John Dickson Carr's biography of Conan Doyle, the author summoned Gillette from London to his place in the country. The two had never met, and Conan Doyle had no idea what Gillette looked like. According to Carr,

> The London train, its green-painted carriages then numbered first and second class, clattered to a stop. And out of it, in a long gray cape, stepped the living image of Sherlock Holmes.

> Not even Sidney Paget had done it so well in a drawing. The clear-cut features, the deep-set eyes, looked out under a deerstalker cap; even Gillette's age, the middle forties, was right.

Conan Doyle was amenable, and by some accounts enthusiastic. With his approval, the play *Sherlock Holmes* was mounted that fall in New York. One of the critics cited Gillette's "scarce gesture and staccato sentence" and agreed with Conan Doyle's assessment that Gillette "looks the part and carries it." The drama was by now an original work, although it included elements from "A Scandal in Bohemia" and "The Final Problem." Another critic called the play "absurd, preposterous and thoroughly delightful." It ran for more than 260 performances in New York, toured the U.S., and then came to London in 1901 (where Charlie Chaplin played the page boy, Billy). It closed after about 200 performances, but was revived with Gillette, now thoroughly identified with the role, in 1905, 1906, 1910, and 1915.

In 1916 there was an American silent film that followed the play closely, starring the now ever-present Gillette. Then in 1923 Gillette revived the play once more and retired.

Gillette had a large body of other work, including plays he wrote for himself that were popular at the time, especially two Civil War melodramas--*Held by the Enemy* and *Secret Service*. He also wrote and appeared in a number of his own comedies, along with works by J. M. Barrie (author of *Peter Pan*) and others.

But he was forever identified in the mind of the theatergoing public with the role of the great detective and in 1929, at the age of seventy-four, Gillette brought Sherlock Holmes back again for a farewell tour of America that would last until 1932.

The Cinematic Holmes

There were a number of early motion pictures featuring Holmes, some of them based on the Gillette play and others adapted or created outright. But given the basic literary form and content of the stories, it was not until the "talk-

Courtesy Foto Fantasies.

Ben Kinglsey as Dr. Watson and Michael Caine as Sherlock Holmes in Without a Clue.
The Museum of Modern Art/Film Stills Archive.

ing picture" era that Sherlock Holmes could emerge as a major figure.

In the early 1930s, as movies began to "speak," well-known actors of the time such as Clive Brook, Reginald Owen, and Raymond Massey played Holmes. But none had the success of Basil Rathbone, whose performances became the touchstone for the character for decades.

Rathbone had been a successful English actor who moved to the United States in the 1920s and became indispensable when the introduction of sound had put many silent screen actors out of work. He appeared in classics such as *David Copperfield, The Adventures of Robin Hood,* and *The Tower of London* and often in the role of villain. Nevertheless, in 1939 he was cast by Twentieth-Century Fox as the Baker Street detective in *The Hound of the Baskervilles* with the English character actor Nigel Bruce as Watson.

The film was a major success, and was followed by a second, *The Adventures of Sherlock Holmes,* which drew both on the stories and Gillette's play, adding many features of its own, particularly an attempt by Professor Moriarty to steal the British crown jewels.

Fox dropped the series, but it was picked up by Universal in 1942 with Rathbone and Bruce continuing their roles. The venue was switched, however, to a contemporary setting, and much of the action was directly tied to the war effort through newly created stories-- *Sherlock Holmes and the Voice of Terror, Sherlock Holmes and the Secret Weapon, Sherlock Holmes in Washington.*

Others were original stories, though

themes and plot items were taken from stories like "The Adventure of the Five Orange Pips" and "The Adventure of the Musgrave Ritual." Rathbone was, in the words of one chronicle, "a convincing, cunning and aloof Sherlock Holmes."

Nigel Bruce's Watson, however, was a rather bumbling assistant, devoted and brave but none too bright (a conception that was to be turned on its head in *Without a Clue,* a 1988 Orion release in which Michael Caine played an incompetent Holmes supported and secretly directed by Ben Kingsley's brilliant Watson).

After the war the Rathbone/Bruce series continued, bringing the total of both Fox and Universal films to fourteen with the last one, *Dressed to Kill* (*Sherlock Holmes and the Secret Code* in the English release).

Rathbone, tired of being identified with the Holmes role, returned to the stage for several years. It was on the stage that he last portrayed Holmes before an audience. In 1953 he appeared on Broadway in a rewritten version of Gillette's play. It closed after only a few performances.

Rathbone then returned to the movies, at first with critical success, including his role as a Boston Brahmin in *The Last Hurrah* in 1958. But he ended his career with appearances in movies like *The Ghost in the Invisible Bikini* and *Hillbillys in a Haunted House.* He died in 1967.

From Wimpole (the Street Where She Lived) to Baker Street

Jeremy Brett, a young English actor with matinee idol good looks, sang "On the Street Where You Live" to an off-screen Eliza Doolittle, in the now classic 1964 Hollywood musical. Few viewers at the time (not to mention Brett himself) could have imagined that the foppish and ineffectual Freddie Einsford-Hill would in a few years be transformed into the most fiercely intellectual and enduring characterization of Sherlock Holmes of the late twentieth century.

And ironically, while the Wimpole Street of *My Fair Lady* was a Hollywood back lot, the real Wimpole Street in London is only a short distance from the Baker Street where Brett would make a much greater mark (although in reality even the Baker Street of the Granada series was a back lot in the northern England city of Manchester).

Peter Jeremy Williams Huggins, who said he took the surname Brett for his career because his army officer father didn't want him to use his real name, had already had a promising career on the London and New York stage when he appeared in the film version of *My Fair Lady.*

A graduate of Eton, he appeared in a supporting role in the 1956 cinema version of *War and Peace* and some low-budget and forgettable English films. But his principal career in the 1950s and '60s was on the English stage, particularly in Shakespearean roles such as Patroclus in *Troilus and Cressida,* Malcolm in *Macbeth,* and the Duke of Aumerle in *Richard II,* roles he repeated in an Old Vic tour of the U.S. and Canada.

He was recast in 1964 with Audrey Hepburn, with whom he had appeared in *War and Peace,* for *My Fair Lady* in

Jeremy Brett in an un-Sherlockian role. Courtesy Museum of Modern Art/Film Stills Archive.

the role of Eliza's feckless, overbred, and unemployable aristocratic suitor. The role did not make Brett a movie star, in part because he went back to England to join Sir Laurence Olivier's National Theater Company.

In the 1970s he appeared in a num-ber of television programs, ranging from quality British efforts like *Rebecca* to American shows such as *Love Boat* and *The Incredible Hulk*. It was in 1978 that he made a further American stage appearance--in the title role of *Dracula* in a play that was produced in Los

Angeles and toured much of the West Coast, and in 1980 in *The Crucifer of Blood,* a Holmes play that was produced in Los Angeles and elsewhere. Brett, however, played Watson to Charlton Heston's Holmes.

He began the Granada television series in 1984. Over the next ten years, with breaks to do other films and a number of plays, he would do a total of forty-one stories.

While the Granada series dramatized the plots, added interpolations and sometimes reworked the order of events, it was notable in that it constituted the first attempt in decades to present all the stories in something like their original form. The great majority of Holmes portrayals on the stage have used the stories more for inspiration than as the firm basis for their plots, and other Holmes theatrical or television movies were either one-time efforts, or so reworked the material that it was only faintly recognizable.

Brett described his own personality as closer to Watson than Holmes, and said Holmes was difficult to play, in part because "he's described by Doyle as man without a heart . . . all brain."

"He's so brilliant, he's so ornate, a boxer, a fencer, he could do everything," Brett said on another occasion. "At the same time, I personally never found him someone I would cross over the road to meet."

Yet he told one newspaper interviewer, "What a role to be typecast in," and one of his breaks from television was as the lead in a stage play called *The Secret*

Nigel Bruce as Watson, Basil Rathborne as Holmes. Courtesy Museum of Modern Art/Film Stills Archive.

of Sherlock Holmes. It enjoyed considerable success in England in the late 1980s but was never produced in the U.S.

While Brett's television performances were generally popular, some critics and members of the public faulted his reliance, particularly in later stories, on tics and other mannerisms to convey emotion. Brett himself struggled with both physical and emotional problems, including manic depression, for which he had been twice hospitalized and about which he was very candid.

Brett died in 1994 in London, leaving nineteen stories yet to be filmed.

The Adventure of the Beryl Coronet

First Publication:

The Strand Magazine, May 1892

Principal Predicament:

When an unnamed man of high rank left England's Beryl Coronet in his care, Alexander Holder, a London banker whose character has never yet borne a stain, decided to place it for safekeeping in the locked bureau in his dressing room. He told only his wayward son Arthur and beloved niece Mary, then went to bed. Shortly, however, he was awakened by a sound and found bad boy Arthur, not only holding the coronet, but attempting to bend it. Arthur turned white and dropped the priceless crown. When the banker discovered that three gems were missing, he accused his son of theft and turned him over to the police. But, where are the missing gems?

Quotable Quote:

Holmes: *"It is an old maxim of mine that when you have excluded the impossible, whatever remains, however improbable, must be the truth."*

Oddities and Discrepancies

Alexander Holder is the senior partner in the second largest private banking concern in London. His son Arthur is a member of an aristocratic club where he's learned to gamble. Given this, it's hard to believe that the good banker would place the valuable gem-laden crown in such an insecure place as an old bureau, and tell his wayward son about it. Even Arthur is surprised by his father's foolishness, exclaiming, "Any old key will fit that bureau."

The Adventure of the Copper Beeches

First Publication:

The Strand Magazine, June 1892

Principal Predicament:

Violet Hunter, a freckle-faced young governess, is broke and desperate for work. A merry, comfortable-looking man makes her an offer she almost can't refuse, but has several firm requests. In return for generous wages, would she live at Copper Beeches, five miles from Winchester? Yes. Take charge of just one "dear little romper," six years old? Yes. Wear any dress her employers chose for her? Yes. Sit where she's told? Yes. Cut her hair very short? No! Miss Hunter begins to suspect that there is something "unnatural" about the terms of her employment. Holmes agrees, telling the governess, "I confess that it is not the situation which I should like to see a sister of mine apply for."

Notable Feature:

Some time before the close of 1891, Conan Doyle wrote his mother that he was thinking of "slaying Holmes in the last and winding him up for good and all. He takes my mind from better things." The Ma'am was horrified and wrote back, reprimanding her son with, "You won't! You can't! You mustn't!" She then suggested he try the plot line she had sent him some time back-- about a golden-haired girl who is kidnapped, shorn of her locks, and made to impersonate another girl for a villainous purpose. Not wanting to offend his mother, Conan Doyle gave it a try and "Copper Beeches" was the result.

The Adventure of Silver Blaze

First Publication:

The Strand Magazine, December 1892

Principal Predicament:

All of England is buzzing about the disappearance of Silver Blaze, the favorite for the Wessex Cup. With the case still unsolved and the race but a few days away, Holmes dons his traveling cap and Watson packs his field glasses, and the two travel to Dartmoor, the sparsely populated heath known for its Gypsy bands and foreboding prison. Not only is the prize-winning horse missing, but his trainer, John Straker, is dead. All bets are off. Or are they? On the night the horse disappeared, someone slipped powdered

A panel by Frank Giacoia for a comic strip version of Silver Blaze. *Credit: Frank Giacoia, Eternity Comics, Malibu Graphics.*

opium into the stableboy's curried mutton. Evidence points toward Fitzroy Simpson, the genteel man of excellent birth and education who has squandered a fortune at the race track. He tried to bribe the maid in the moor that dark night and it's his silk cravat the dead man clutches. By tale's end, Colonel Ross, the horse's wealthy owner, and Inspector Gregory, the officer assigned to the case, are of less help to Holmes in solving the mystery than are the animals—the dog who didn't bark, the lame sheep in the paddock, and the horse, of course.

Notable Features:

Holmes admits to making a "blunder." He also indulges in a little gambling. This story is also notable because Watson sees something significant before Holmes does. "One for you, Watson," says Holmes, giving credit where credit is due.

Quotable Quotes:

Inspector Gregory: *"Is there any other point to which you would wish to draw my attention?"* Holmes: *"To the curious incident of the dog in the night-time."* Gregory: *"The dog did nothing in the night-time."* Holmes: *"That was the curious incident."*

The Adventure of the Cardboard Box

First Publication:

The Strand Magazine, January 1893

Principal Predicament:

Susan Cushing, a placid-faced maiden lady of fifty, has received a gruesome packet in the mail containing two human ears. Holmes, called into the case by Inspector Lestrade of Scotland Yard, observes immediately that the freshly severed ears are from different heads. Though both ears are pierced for an earring, one is a woman's small, finely formed ear, while the other is an ear from a man who has been in the sun a great deal. Lestrade is inclined to believe this is a practical joke played on a woman who has led a quiet and respectable life. Holmes, however, believes a double murder has been committed. "There is a tangle here which needs straightening out," he says ominously.

Notable Feature:

Conan Doyle tried to suppress this story after its initial publication, believing it to be, not only grim and gruesome, but sensational because of the sexual indiscretion in the plot. Consequently, the story was not included in *The Memoirs of Sherlock Holmes,* the second set of collected cases. Later, the author had an apparent change of heart and allowed the story to be included in *His Last Bow,* a collection of stories published in 1917. One consequence of this convoluted publishing history is that the famous mind-reading scene, initially part of "Cardboard Box," was incorporated into another story, "The Adventure of the Resident Patient," and then moved back again. In an American edition of *The Complete Sherlock Holmes,* the episode appears in both stories.

"He took out the two ears as he spoke, and laying a board across his knee, he examined them minutely . . ."

Title Nouns and Adjectives

Connect these title nouns and adjectives:

CROOKED	Client
CREEPING	Detective
DYING	Soldier
DANCING	House
MISSING	Man
EMPTY	Patient
SOLITARY	Lodger
VEILED	Man
BLANCHED	Three-Quarter
ILLUSTRIOUS	Interpreter
RESIDENT	Cyclist
GREEK	Men

Solutions: CROOKED-*Man*; CREEPING-*Man*; DYING-*Detective*; DANCING-*Men*; MISSING-*Three-Quarter*; EMPTY-*House*; SOLITARY-*Cyclist*; VEILED-*Lodger*; BLANCHED-*Soldier*; ILLUSTRIOUS-*Client*; RESIDENT-*Patient*; GREEK-*Interpreter*.

Why the Long Face? Sherlock Holmes and the Pursuit of Pleasure

——◦◦◦——

Sherlock Holmes has frequently been portrayed as an austere and humorless man. He postures as an ascetic figure, with a disinclination toward anything the rest of us might consider fun and a disregard for personal comfort.

In truth, he is a free spirit who joyfully indulges in a range of pleasures. Unfettered by social constraints and expectations, he boldly feasts on the whole banquet of life, savoring what is most highly spiced.

Our very first image of Holmes at St. Bartholomew's chemical laboratory is of a delighted detective, not a grim one. Even before the future flatmates are introduced by young Stamford, Watson sees Holmes spring to his feet and hears his "cry of pleasure." Immediately after the two shake hands and exchange greetings, Holmes "chuckles to himself." Before they leave the lab, Watson again hears Holmes cry, "Ha! ha!" and sees him clap his hands. Watson notes that Holmes, absorbed in a chemistry experiment, looks as "delighted as a child

with a new toy." After their historic meeting, Watson describes Holmes as having eyes that fairly glittered and a merry laugh.

A merry laugh? Yes. It is Holmes, the light-hearted Londoner, who, in "The Adventure of the Mazarin Stone," cries out, "Why not give ourselves up to the unrestrained enjoyment of the present?" albeit at the time being held at gunpoint. Moments later he has cause to remark, "I have an impish habit of practical joking."

Watson is partly responsible for the false perception of Holmes as humorless. When, for example, the doctor refers to the detective's "somber and cynical spirit," as he does in "The Adventure of the Devil's Foot," he disguises the truth, which is that Sherlock Holmes is a true bon vivant, albeit a moody and mercurial one. Several students of the Canon have analyzed the lighter side of the detective's personality. In their essay entitled, "The Man Who Seldom Laughed," Charles and Edward Lauterbach actually catalogued Holmes's indicators of pleasure and found that, in the Canon, he smiles 103 times, jokes 58 times, chuckles 31 times, laughs another 65 times, and displays general good humor 59 times for a grand total of 316 examples of pleasure.

Watson is just wrong when he describes Holmes as taking little interest in his own comfort. Just the opposite is true. Holmes indulges his every desire, including his desire to brood and sulk.

The confusion comes because Watson's definition of comfort is not Holmes's. For the more pedestrian doctor, as for most of us, the notion of comfort brings to mind images of home and family, friends, good food, warm beds, and such, but Holmes is an eccentric and his notion of comfort falls outside the normal parameters.

Watson constantly marvels at their dissimilar notion of pleasure. When he laments that a depleted bank account will cause him to postpone his August holiday and the chance to escape London's heat, he contrasts his disappointment with Holmes's contentment, writing, "As to my companion, neither the country nor the sea presented the slightest attraction to him. He loved to lie in the very center of five millions of people, with his filaments stretching out and running through them, responsive to every little rumor or suspicion of unsolved crime."

Though his idea of how to have a good time may be unconventional,

---

"As a rule, the more bizarre a thing is the less mysterious it proves to be. It is your commonplace, featureless crimes which are really puzzling, just as a commonplace face is the most difficult to identify."
—*The Red-Headed League*

Holmes knows what he wants, nor will he deprive himself. He operates on the assumption that he is entitled to an interesting life. Not for him, the daily grind of routine at work or home. Not for him, playing the game of pleasing others. No, for Holmes, the only game is the one of his own choosing. When he wishes to sleep in the morning, he does. When he wishes to practice with his revolver, he does that too–even if it means shooting a crisp "V.R." (Victoria Regina) into his landlady's wall.

His bold grasp on the lapels of life is part of this detective's universal appeal. In an essay, Edgar W. Smith wrote of Sherlock Holmes, "He is Galahad and Socrates, bringing high adventure to our dull existences and calm, judicial logic to our biased minds. He is the success of all our failures; the bold escape from our imprisonment."

From Extreme Languor to Devouring Energy

Idleness is anathema to Holmes. He goes to great lengths to avoid it and when faced with it, does little to keep up appearances. Instead, he gives in to the exhaustion idleness induces and spends whole days in bed, sometimes "hardly uttering a word or moving a muscle from morning to night." "My mind rebels at stagnation," he pouts, steadfast in his efforts "to escape from the commonplaces of existence."

Holmes is a responsibility-free adult at liberty to indulge his whims, his vices, his temptations, all with a minimum of guilt or consequences. When he needs to brood, simply staring into space is not enough; he turns to drugs.

In "A Scandal in Bohemia," Watson writes that, "Holmes, who loathed every form of society with his whole Bohemian soul, remained in our lodgings in Baker Street, buried among his old books, and alternating from week to week between cocaine and ambition, the drowsiness of the drug, and the fierce energy of his own keen nature."

Neither hunger nor fatigue can discourage the engrossed sleuth when he has a case to occupy his mind. He genuinely loves a challenge and thrives on problem solving. Watson, watching from a distance like a worried parent, is relieved when he sees Holmes pacing in "A Scandal in Bohemia":

> His rooms were brilliantly lit, and, even as I looked up, I saw his tall, spare figure pass twice in a dark silhouette against the blind. He was pacing the room swiftly, eagerly, with his head sunk upon his chest and his hands clasped behind him. To me, who knew his every mood and habit, his attitude and manner told their own story. He was at work again. He had risen out of his drug-created dreams and was hot upon the scent of some new problem.

Miserable when all the pieces fit too easily, his good nature is stimulated by matters amiss. So writes his scribe in "The Adventure of the Missing Three-Quarter," "A cold supper was ready upon the table, and when his needs were satisfied and his pipe alight, he was ready to take that half comic and wholly philosophic view which was natural to him when his affairs were going awry."

Work, however, is just one of the distractions Holmes employs to appease his restless soul and curious mind. The sleuth has a range of interests and activities to enliven even his bleakest moods.

The Charm of Music

It is not uncommon for Holmes, in the thick of the chase, to stop everything for a trip to the concert hall. Anticipating a late night of crime solving in "The Red-Headed League," Holmes seizes the day, saying, "A sandwich, and a cup of coffee, and then off to violin land, where all is sweetness, and delicacy, and harmony, and there are no red-headed clients to vex us with their conundrums." As Watson describes Holmes later that day:

> All the afternoon he sat in the stalls wrapped in the most perfect happiness, gently waving his long thin fingers in time to the music, while his gently smiling face and his languid, dreamy eyes were as unlike those of Holmes the sleuth-hound, Holmes the relentless, keen-witted, ready-handed criminal agent, as it was possible to conceive.

In "The Adventure of the Cardboard Box," when Holmes and Watson are denied permission to visit Sarah Cushing, the detective quickly concedes, cheerfully saying, "Well, if we can't, we can't." The doctor and detective then share a pleasant little meal, during which Holmes talks of nothing but violins and of Paganini, the celebrated Italian violinist. Writes Watson, "We sat for an hour over a bottle of claret while he told me anecdote after anecdote of that extraordinary man."

A patron of the opera, German music is more to his taste than Italian or French. Holmes not only listens but enjoys studying music. In November 1895, as a dense yellow fog invades London, Holmes occupies his time with a new hobby, studying the music of the Middle Ages.

Just days later he takes a day off from his search for the Bruce-Partington plans to work on a monograph about the obscure polyphonic motets of Orlando Lassus, a composer of the sixteenth century. As soon as the lost plans are found and the mystery is solved, Holmes returns, refreshed, to his work on Lassus, and when this monograph is eventually published it is said by the experts to be the last word upon the subject.

In *A Study in Scarlet,* Holmes takes time out during the Drebber investigation to attend a concert by Wilhelmine Norman-Neruda, the Austrian violinist, about whom he says, "her attack and her bowing are splendid." Watson adds in his notes, "Leaning back in the cab, this amateur bloodhound carolled away like a lark while I meditated upon the manysidedness of the human mind."

At the end of *The Hound of the Baskervilles,* Holmes says, "And now, my dear Watson, we have had some weeks of severe work, and for one evening, I think, we may turn our thoughts into more pleasant channels. I have a box for *Les Huguenots.* Have you heard the De Reszkes?" The De Reszkes were two Polish brothers who sang with the Metropolitan Opera in New York. That Holmes has secured a box at the opera only reinforces the fact that he does not neglect his love of music, but takes advantage of life in the big city.

Not satisfied with listening alone, he is "a composer of no ordinary merit," and a capable performer as well. His chosen instrument is the violin, and not just any violin, but the best—a prized Stradivarius. With the violin case propped in its accustomed place, a corner of the Baker Street room, upon request Holmes can play the difficult "Lieder" by Mendelssohn. He plays at strange hours, unconcerned about disturbing his neighbors or landlady. Sometimes, playing is a solace, as it is during his dealings in "The Five Orange Pips" when he concedes, "There is nothing more to be said or to be done tonight, so hand me over my violin and let us try to forget for half an hour the miserable weather and the still more miserable ways of our fellowmen."

Often, he plays to express his moods, not necessarily anything with a recognizable melody, but wordless, tuneless sounds that express his inner thoughts, as he's described in *A Study in Scarlet.* "Leaning back in his armchair of an evening, he would close his eyes and scrape carelessly at the fiddle which was thrown across his knee. Sometimes the chords were sonorous and melancholy. Occasionally they were fantastic and cheerful."

Quite a Three-Pipe Problem

"You don't mind the smell of strong tobacco, I hope?" Holmes asks Watson

"It is quite a three-pipe problem."
Illustration by Andrew Glass for a book of
Sherlock Holmes stories adapted for young
readers. Credit: © Andrew Glass, 1981

My first impression as I opened the door was that a fire had broken out, for the room was so filled with smoke that the light of the lamp upon the table was blurred by it. As I entered, however my fears were set at rest, for it was the acrid fumes of strong coarse tobacco which took me by the throat and set me coughing. Through the haze I had a vague vision of Holmes in his dressing-gown coiled up in an armchair with his black clay pipe between his lips.

"Caught cold, Watson?" said he.

"No, it's this poisonous atmosphere."

"I suppose it *is* pretty thick, now that you mention it."

"Thick! It is intolerable."

in their get-acquainted interview, and for good reason. Holmes is, by any reckoning, a heavy smoker, and though Watson treats the seemingly innocent question with a comradely shrug, he is soon disapproving of Holmes's indulgence, labelling Holmes "a self-poisoner by cocaine and tobacco." These are strong words in the smoking-lenient, polluted London of the late nineteenth century.

As inevitably as the dense fog will roll down the streets of London, so a thick cloud of smoke will fill the Baker Street flat. At one point in *The Hound of the Baskervilles,* Holmes is in need of seclusion and solitude for intense mental concentration on the problem at hand. But when Watson returns to the Baker Street rooms that evening he is, at first, alarmed:

Smoking is an art form as practiced by Holmes. A litter of pipes and tobacco pouches are strewn everywhere. Holmes's choice of tobacco is shag, a strong, coarsely cut leaf, which he orders by the pound from Bradley, Watson's tobacconist. He keeps his tobacco in the toe-end of a Persian slipper and his cigars in the coal scuttle.

Holmes has different pipes for different moods. When he is feeling argumentative he smokes his *cherry wood.* Occasionally he smokes his *amber stem* and other times his *brier.* His *before breakfast pipe,* which he smokes in his sitting room while wearing a dressing gown and reading the agony column of *The Times,* is stuffed with "all the plugs and dottles left from his smokes of the day before, all carefully dried and collected on the corner of the mantelpiece."

His *clay pipe* has a special function; it helps him think. More than once, Watson describes Holmes's use of this pipe as a meditative tool, as he does in "A Case of Identity": "He took down from the rack the old and oily clay pipe, which was to him as a counselor, and, having lit it he leaned back in his chair, with the thick blue cloud-wreaths spinning up from him, and a look of infinite languor in his face."

Smoking is part and parcel of his way of being, his modus operandi, his detective's art. "It is quite a three-pipe problem," Holmes tells Watson as he curls himself up in his chair to think over the curious doings of the League of Red-Headed Men, "his black clay pipe thrusting out like the bill of some strange bird."

Though he smokes in forty-nine of the sixty stories, there is no mention of a pipe with a curved stem, such as the one introduced into the public imagination as a Holmesian trademark by the American actor William Gillette. In fact, such pipes were largely unknown in England until the Boer War, circa 1899.

Holmes does more than smoke tobacco, of course; he studies it. He brags to Watson, "I flatter myself that I can distinguish at a glance the ash of any known brand either of cigar or of tobacco." More than once he refers to the monograph he has written titled "Upon the Distinction between the Ashes of the Various Tobaccos." He says, "In it I enumerate a hundred and forty forms of cigar, cigarette, and pipe tobacco, with colored plates illustrating the difference in the ash." To which Watson, in admirable understatement,

says, "You have an extraordinary genius for minutiae."

You're One That Has Wasted Your Gifts

Though it is a mystery how Holmes keeps up his athletic skills, since he seldom takes exercise for exercise's sake, we know from Watson's testimony that he is physically fit: "Few men were capable of greater muscular effort." In *The Sign of the Four*, when Holmes encounters McMurdo, the former prizefighter and servant to Bartholomew Sholto, he genially reminds the deep-chested boxer that they know each other:

> I don't think you can have forgotten me. Don't you remember the amateur who fought three rounds with you at Alison's rooms on the night of your benefit four years back?

To which the boxer replies:

> Not Mr. Sherlock Holmes! . . . God's truth! how could I have mistook you? If instead o' standin' there so quiet you had just stepped up and given me that cross-hit of yours under the jaw, I'd ha' known you without a question. Ah, you're one that has wasted your gifts, you have! You might have aimed high, if you had joined the fancy.

While Watson's game is rugby, Holmes is not a team player. He prefers solitary sports like swimming and fishing or the one-on-one sport of fencing. He's an expert at singlestick. In "The Adventure of the Illustrious Client," when he's hospitalized after being savagely assaulted by two men armed with sticks, he reassures Watson, "Don't look so scared . . . It's not as bad as it seems . . . I'm a bit of a singlestick expert, as you know. I took most of them on my guard."

Knowledge of Japanese wrestling actually saves the detective's life when he encounters Professor Moriarty at Reichenbach Falls. As he tells Watson;

> We tottered together upon the brink of the fall. I have some knowledge, however, of baritsu, or the Japanese system of wrestling, which has more than once been very useful to me. I slipped through his grip, and he with a horrible scream kicked madly for a few seconds and clawed the air with both his hands.

Reading, Writing, and Chemistry

"I am an omnivorous reader with a strangely retentive memory for trifles," says Holmes in "The Adventure of the Lion's Mane." Throughout the Canon, he quotes Shakespeare (badly) and the Bible (fairly). On the train to the Boscombe Valley, he pulls out his pocket-sized volume of works by Petrarch, the fourteenth century Italian poet, while, during that same venture, Watson reads a "yellow-backed novel."

In *The Sign of the Four*, Holmes says, "Goethe is always pithy," quoting the German poet, not once but twice. In the same story he and Watson discuss another German writer, Richter, while in hot pursuit, with the dog Toby, down

half-rural villa-lined roads on the hunt for felons.

Again in *The Sign of the Four*, we get a glimpse of how Holmes has spent his leisure time when he sits down to a "merry" meal in a state of nervous exaltation. Watson writes,

> I have never know him so brilliant. He spoke on a quick succession of subjects—on miracle plays, on medieval pottery, on Stradivarius violins, on the Buddhism of Ceylon, and

on the warships of the future—handling each as though he had made a special study of it. His bright humor marked the reaction from his black depression of the preceding days.

Indeed, Holmes probably has made a special study of these topics for, in addition to being a reader, he is also a writer of some note, having published numerous monographs on a range of subjects–from an essay on the Chaldean roots of the Cornish language to two short articles on human ears (published in the *Anthropological Journal*). Of course, in keeping with his line of work, he has also written about tattoos, the tracing of footsteps, and the uses of dogs in the work of the detective.

Petrarch and Goethe aside, Holmes is a faithful reader of the newspaper's "agony column" (akin to our personal ads). "What a chorus of groans, cries, and bleatings!" Holmes laments in "The Adventure of the Red Circle." He not only reads the "cipher messages" but occasionally plants a few of his own to lure unsuspecting readers into revealing either their knowledge or their ignorance of the mystery at hand.

Untold hours of concentrated work occupy the detective as he clips the paper and pastes items of interest into his "Commonplace Book," actually a series of scrapbooks all carefully (though unconventionally) indexed. How better to spend a stormy September night than by indexing?

Some of Holmes's happiest moments are those spent bent over his chemistry experiments. According to Watson's notes on "The Adventure of the Musgrave Ritual," the Baker Street rooms "were always full of chemicals and of criminal relics, which had a way of wandering into unlikely positions, and of turning up in the butter-dish, or in even less desirable places." (One might wonder what a less desirable place might be to find a wandering relic than a butter-dish!)

In the opening of "The Adventure of the Dancing Men" Watson describes Holmes seated before his test tubes. "Holmes had been seated for some hours in silence with his long, thin back curved over a chemical vessel in which he was brewing a particularly malodorous product. His head was sunk upon his breast, and he looked from my point of view like a strange, lank bird, with dull gray plumage and a black top-knot."

The Ordinary Is Extraordinary

For one with a restless mind, the ordinary is extraordinary, and challenges abound in every nook and cranny, and so, the great detective plays endless games with himself. He memorizes the order of houses along the streets of his city and explains to Watson, "It is a hobby of mine to have an exact knowledge of London."

Holmes also knows something about playing cards. Preparing for the long hours of waiting he anticipates at the conclusion of "The Red-Headed League," Holmes has in his pocket, not a gun, but a pack of cards, betraying more than a superficial interest in the game.

One glance at Holmes's Baker Street rooms reveals the diverse hobbies of this solitary man and shows us what he loves and cares about, what pieces of the world he chooses to keep at his tobacco-stained fingertips. Watson sees that room with fresh eyes when he enters after an agonized absence in "The Adventure of the Empty House."

As I entered I saw, it is true, an unwonted tidiness, but the old landmarks were all in their place. There were the chemical corner and the acid-stained, deal-topped table. There upon a shelf was the row of formidable scrapbooks and books of reference which many of our fellow-citizens would have been so glad to burn. The diagrams, the violin-case, and the pipe-rack–even the Persian slipper which contained the tobacco–all met my eyes as I glanced round me.

Beauty, Hope, and Holmes

Finally, this man Holmes, who claims again and again to be all brain, betrays himself to have a great appreciation for the ungraspables of life–hope and beauty. Twice in "The Adventure of the Naval Treaty," he drops the pretense of bleak despair he so enjoys, first when gently holding in his hands a dainty moss rose, all crimson and green. "What a lovely thing a rose is!" he sighs, lost in a reverie, then says:

> Our highest assurance of the goodness of Providence seems to me to rest in the flowers. All other things, our powers, our desires, our food, are all really necessary for our existence in the first instance. But this rose is an extra. Its smell and its color are an embellishment of life, not a condition of it. It is only goodness which gives extras, and so I say again that we have much to hope from the flowers.

What is even more profound and touching is the hope for humanity Holmes expresses on the train back into the city, when he tells Watson, "It's a very cheery thing to come into London by any of these lines which run high and allow you to look down upon the houses like this." Watson thinks Holmes is joking for, to him, the scene is sordid. But Holmes is joyful, seeing the new "board schools" or public academies, which loom above the housetops of the city:

> Light-houses, my boy! Beacons of the future! Capsules with hundreds of bright little seeds in each, out of which will spring the wiser, better England of the future.

This is Sherlock Holmes, optimist and bon vivant, the lover of life.

Not So Elementary, My Dear Watson

Surely one of Sherlock Holmes's most famous statements is the rejoinder–"Elementary, my dear Watson!" Unfortunately, this statement appears nowhere in the Canon.

Holmes did have a habit of saying "elementary," most often when a stunned listener claimed to be astonished by one of his remarkable deductions. Sometimes, though, instead of saying "elementary," Holmes would utter other exclamations such as "simplicity itself" or "commonplace" or sometimes even "absurdly commonplace."

The sentiment, if not the words, "elementary, my dear Watson" is repeated throughout the Canon. In the opening scene of "A Scandal in Bohemia," Watson is bewildered by a deduction made by Holmes. "My dear Holmes . . . this is too much. You would certainly have been burned, had you lived a few centuries ago." Holmes chuckles and replies casually, "It is simplicity itself." He then proceeds to chide Watson saying, "You see, but you do not observe"–an accusation Holmes was to make numerous times.

The most stupefying deduction is

Holmes astonished Watson with his observation, "Your eyes flashed across to the unframed portrait of Henry Ward Beecher which stands upon the top of your books. Then you glanced up at the wall, and of course your meaning was obvious."

made at the beginning of "The Adventure of the Cardboard Box." Holmes seems preoccupied, so Watson, having finished reading the paper, lets his mind wander aimlessly until Holmes interrupts with, "You are right, Watson. . . . It does seem a very preposterous way of settling a dispute." Holmes has seemingly read Watson's mind, plucked his unspoken thoughts right out of the air. The bewildered doctor sputters, "This is beyond anything which I could have imagined." Holmes laughs and proceeds to describe Watson's long, meandering train of thought, from his contemplation of the framed picture of General Gordon and the unframed portrait of Henry Ward Beecher (revealed by the movement of Watson's eyes) to his musings on war's useless waste of life (revealed by the motion of his hand toward his old war wound–wherever that might be).

At the opening of "The Adventure of the Dancing Men," we find Watson once again sputtering with astonishment over a Holmesian insight into his unspoken thoughts. This time, Holmes has been bent over a test tube in silence for some hours, when he suddenly speaks, out of the blue, "So, Watson, you do not propose to invest in South African securities?" This, as it turns out, was just what Watson was pondering. The subsequent conversation reveals the humor Holmes takes in what he knows is not at all an "elementary" talent for deduction.

"How on earth do you know that?" I asked.

He wheeled round upon his stool, with a steaming test-tube in his hand,

and a gleam of amusement in his deep-set eyes.

"Now, Watson, confess yourself utterly taken aback," said he.

"I am."

"I ought to make you sign a paper to that effect."

"Why?"

"Because in five minutes you will say that it is all so absurdly simple."

"I am sure that I shall say nothing of the kind."

But, of course, Watson does wind up saying, " How absurdly simple!"

In "The Disappearance of Lady Frances Carfax," Watson foolishly thinks, albeit for only a moment, that he has caught Holmes in an erroneous deduction. The story opens with Holmes gazing at Watson's boots and asking, "But why Turkish?" Watson, surprised, responds that the boots are English. Holmes, it turns out, was not referring to Watson's boots, but to the kind of bath Watson has had. Watson, then, says, "I have no doubt the connection between my boots and a Turkish bath is a perfectly self-evident one to a logical mind, and yet I should be obliged to you if you would indicate it." Holmes responds with a decided twinkle in his eye, "The train of reasoning is not very obscure, Watson." This tête-à-tête is the familiar one–from Watson's bafflement to Holmes's post explanation comment on the simplicity of his deductions, "Absurd, is it not?"

Does Holmes ever actually say, "elementary, my dear Watson" all in one phrasing? No. Like the deerstalker and the curved pipe, the famous phrase is "non-canonical," which means it does not appear in the actual stories as written by Sir Arthur Conan Doyle. We must settle for some close couplings of the word "elementary" with the affectionate, if condescending, "my dear Watson."

In *The Hound of the Baskervilles*, the words "elementary" and "my dear Watson" appear just sentences apart. Watson has tried his hand at deduction, in this case attempting to draw conclusions from the walking stick left behind by a visitor. After a valiant attempt by the good doctor, Holmes takes a look. "Interesting, though elementary," he concludes, then lands a blow. "I am afraid, my dear Watson, that most of your conclusions were erroneous."

In "The Adventure of the Crooked Man," Holmes addresses his friend as "my dear Watson" and just a few sentences later says to him, "elementary."

This close coupling of the two key parts of the famous phrase comes after Holmes comments innocently that the newly married Watson has been professionally rather busy of late. Watson confirms the observation but says, "I don't know how you deduced it."

But the closest we come to the famous yet unspoken phrase is in one of the last stories of the Canon, "The Adventure of the Retired Colourman." Watson has just given a long, detailed report of his day's observations and has mentioned seeing a tall, dark man, when Holmes pipes up, "No doubt! No doubt! . . . A tall, dark, heavily moustached man, you say, with gray-tinted sun-glasses?" Watson, as astonished as ever, sputters "Holmes, you are a wizard. I did not say so, but he *had* gray-tinted sun-glasses." "And a Masonic tie-pin?" asks Holmes. "Holmes!" pants the dumbfounded doctor—to which the amused Holmes responds, "Quite simple, my dear Watson." But not, alas, "elementary."

The Adventure of the Yellow Face

First Publication:

The Strand Magazine, February 1893

Principal Predicament:

Grant Munro thought he and his wife Effie were happily married, until she suddenly began asking for money and visiting the newly occupied cottage nearby at all hours of the day and night. When asked, she refused to explain her behavior. There is obviously a growing secret between husband and wife. The bewildered husband only grows more concerned when he sees a yellow face in the window. There is something unnatural and inhuman about the face, he says. Upon entering his neighbor's cottage, Grant finds a large picture of his wife on the mantelpiece. He wants answers. The only bit of unusual history he knows about Effie is that she once lived in America where her first husband and her baby both died in a yellow fever epidemic. Upon hearing this, Holmes fashions a theory that, after a good laugh and a happy ending, turns out to be wrong.

Notable Feature:

Holmes jumps to some erroneous conclusions in this case and eats humble pie quite modestly at story's end.

Quotable Quote:

Holmes: *"If it should ever strike you that I am getting a little over-confident in my powers, or giving less pains to a case than it deserves, kindly whisper 'Norbury' in my ear, and I shall be infinitely obliged to you."*

ODDITIES AND DISCREPANCIES:

Effie says she was married while in the United States and lived in the town of Atlanta. Readers may assume the American locale was the city in Georgia, but at the story's conclusion, those with knowledge of Southern law and history are likely to conclude it must have been another Atlanta.

Above: Effie Munro pulled at her husband's sleeve with convulsive strength and cried,
"I swear that I will tell you everything some day . . ."
Illustration by William H. Hyde for Harper's Weekly, *February 1893.*

C A P S U L E

The Adventure of the Stock-Broker's Clerk

First Publication:

The Strand Magazine, March 1893

Principal Predicament:

Hall Pycroft, an up-and-coming young clerk with a frank, honest face full of cheeriness, laments as the story begins: "I show myself up as such a confounded fool!" He's been persuaded to ignore an offer of employment from one of the richest stockbroking firms in London and to spend his days, instead, working for the Birmingham office of a new firm named the Franco-Midland Hardware Company. He's begun to feel uneasy around Arthur Pinner, the London-based financial agent whose cheeks are the dull, dead white of a fish's belly, and his brother Harry Pinner. Why have they dragged him out to Birmingham? Where is everyone else who works for Franco-Midland Hardware? And how can they afford to pay him the princely sum of £500 a year, more than twice his previous offer?

Notable Feature:

There's an anti-Semitic description of villain Arthur Pinner as having "a touch of the sheeny about his nose." And some readers have wondered about the necessity of the elaborate stratagem of one man trying to masquerade as two, claiming that the plot would have worked as well with just one proprietor of Franco-Midland Hardware.

C A P S U L E

The Adventure of the "Gloria Scott"

First Publication:

The Strand Magazine, April 1893

Principal Predicament:

Holmes tells Watson about his very first case. As a university student, he had gone home with his college pal for a holiday in Norfolk. Old Trevor, the friend's father, had very little book-learning, but had traveled extensively and, though burly and weather-beaten, had a reputation for kindness. One sunny day, Old Trevor had a visitor—a wizened little seaman with a crafty face and badly worn boots. He said his name was Hudson. An hour after his arrival, he was dead drunk. The next day, Holmes left for London, but a telegram from his friend a few weeks later took him back to Norfolk where he was met with the news that Old Trevor seemed about to die of nervous shock. Hudson, the seaman from Old Trevor's past, had finally been asked to leave after several weeks of outrageous behavior. Then, a letter had arrived with these words: "The supply of game for London is going steadily up. Head-keeper Hudson, we believe, has been now told to receive all orders for fly-paper and for preservation of your hen-pheasant's life." What could it mean?

Oddities and Discrepancies:

What university did Holmes attend—Oxford, Cambridge, or somewhere else? The debate rages fiercely among Sherlockians around the world.

A very young Holmes astonished Old Trevor with his deductions. Illustration by William H. Hyde for Harper's Weekly, *April 1893.*

The Adventure of the Musgrave Ritual

First Publication:

The Strand Magazine, May 1893

Principal Predicament:

Unfortunately for Reginald Musgrave, the pale, aristocratic master of the Manor House of Hurlstone who knew Holmes from their college days, his servants have more curiosity and intelligence than he has. When he finds his handsome butler, Brunton, pawing through some private family papers, he fires him on the spot, though the man has been an invaluable employee for twenty years. Musgrave gives the man a week to pack his bags, but the disgraced Brunton suddenly disappears after only two days, leaving behind his money, his watch, his boots. Soon after, the distraught, jilted maid, Rachel Howells, disappears too. The lake is dragged for bodies, but yields only a linen bag containing an odd assortment of items—a mass of old rusted metal and several dull-colored pieces of pebble or glass. Holmes determines that a family ritual holds the key. He studies the strange catechism beginning with the first question: "Whose was it?" Answer: "His who is gone."

". . . when Holmes in one of his queer humours would sit in an arm-chair, with his hair-trigger and a hundred Boxer cartridges, and proceed to adorn the opposite wall with a patriotic V.R. done in bullet-pocks, I felt strongly that neither the atmosphere nor the appearance of our room was improved by it."

Notable Features:

This case is recounted as an early one presented by a personal acquaintance in the days before he met Watson, when he had rooms in Montague Street. Also, Watson describes the unsettling and untidy habits of his fellow lodger, including the way he sits in an armchair with his pistol. Once, Holmes even "adorned the opposite wall with a patriotic V.R." (that's Victoria Regina).

Oddities and Discrepancies:

Musgrave claims that, after the butler disappeared, he had the estate thoroughly searched. "We ransacked every room and cellar without discovering the least sign of the missing man." How is it, then, that Musgrave leads Holmes to a cellar and is surprised to find the butler's muffler attached to an iron ring in the center of the heavy flagstone?

"Save for the Occasional Use of Cocaine, He Had No Vices. . . ."

Although such a statement as Watson's in "The Adventure of the Yellow Face" would now be regarded as absurd or ironic, in Conan Doyle's day, drug addiction was not well understood, and patent medicines containing opiates and stimulants—and even the drugs themselves—were available to everyone without prescription. Their use was widespread until they were made illegal in the first decades of the twentieth century.

Watson's concern over Holmes's drug use was profound, but at the time he and others regarded such drugs with the caution we would now associate with powerful legal medications, rather than as outlaw substances.

Opium, a derivative of the poppy, had been available in England at least since the fourteenth century, and in the centuries immediately prior to the Victorian era had become more and more common. In 1680 an English apothecary introduced a mixture of wine, spices, and opium as Sydenham's Laudanum. Other patent medicines followed, including Dover's Powder, a remedy for the then common and painful ailment of gout. Thomas Dover cited "the extraordinary refreshment of spirits" brought about by his opium mixture, and the use of patent medicines containing opium spread to all classes.

This was due in no small part to the limited state of the medical profession even as late as Watson's era. While medical knowledge had steadily increased, there was little or nothing doctors could do about many major and potentially fatal ailments, including what we would now regard as minor infections.

Thus people routinely treated themselves for illnesses, using herbal remedies or animal and mineral compounds reputed to have some curative power. And unlike many nostrums of that period, opium actually was effective, particularly when used to relieve severe pain and to stop coughing and diarrhea (purposes opiates retain today in prescription medications).

Opium's mood-elevating effects obviously did not go unnoticed, and by

An opium den.

the early nineteenth century, it was becoming clear that overdependence on opiates could produce lethargy and depression, and more horrifying symptoms when the drug became unavailable. In 1822 Thomas De Quincey, who had started taking laudanum for a gastric ulcer and became addicted, published (anonymously) *Confessions of an English Opium Eater* and outlined both the joys and sorrows of opium use.

His friend and neighbor in England's Lake District, Samuel Taylor Coleridge, was also an opium addict, and the drug's occasional psychedelic effects are generally cited in works like his famous poem "Kubla Khan." Coleridge strug-

"There is nothing more deceptive than an obvious fact."
—*The Boscombe Valley Mystery*

gled with his dependence on the drug for most of his adult life. Wilkie Collins, author of *The Moonstone,* used opium addiction as a plot device in this groundbreaking detective tale. It was said to echo in some respects his own addiction.

Chasing the Dragon

Although Holmes used injections, opium was most often taken by Victorians in pills, preparations, or even wine. The habit of smoking it (though opium inhalation had been introduced to China by Europeans in the seventeenth century) was regarded as a somewhat degraded Oriental vice.

The opium den was a standard element in sensational literature of the day, both journalistic and fictional. Conan Doyle used it in "The Man with the Twisted Lip," where early in the story Watson finds himself in The Bar of Gold on Upper Swandam Lane, "a vile alley lurking behind the wharves which line the north side of the river to the east end of London Bridge."

Retrieving a friend and patient, Isa Whitney, from what Holmes describes as "the vilest murder trap on the whole riverside," Watson describes entering "a long, low room, thick and heavy with the brown opium smoke." His friend Whitney, having spent two days there "among the dregs of the docks," was "in a pitiable state . . . pale, haggard and unkempt," and "sank his face onto his arms and began to sob in a high treble key."

In the Arms of Morpheus

While opium had been known for centuries, morphine was a nineteenth century creation, chemically extracted from opium and used for many of the same purposes. Physicians preferred it because as a manufactured substance its quality was more uniform and the effects of its dosages more predictable.

It was widely used in the care of the wounded during the American Civil War, producing a postwar crop of addicted veterans. Heroin, which does not figure in the Canon, was a further refinement of opium, and was originally considered a nonaddicting treatment for opium/morphine addiction.

Cocaine Blues

While opium and its derivatives are classified as narcotics, cocaine is pharmaceutically a stimulant. "I abhor the dull routine of existence. I crave for mental exaltation," Holmes cries as he prepares a "seven-per-cent solution" for self-injection in The Sign of the Four.

He was not alone.

Preparations based on the South American coca leaf had taken the United States and Europe by storm in the last half of the nineteenth century, often through the use of a mixture of alcohol and coca. One such, marketed as Vin Mariani (after its inventor, a Corsican chemist named Angelo Mariani) became so popular as a tonic and then a recreational drink that it earned testimonials from Thomas Edison, Jules Verne, Alexandre Dumas, and Pope Leo XIII, among others.

Its success helped inspire many imitators. Among them was the American John Styth Pemberton, who in 1885 registered a trademark for French Wine Cola. Partially to appease prohibition interests, he later changed the wine to a caffeine base and marketed it as "Coca-Cola–an intellectual beverage and temperance drink."

Coca leaf had been used for centuries in the Andes. The chemical extraction of the leaf's most potent alkaloids was not accomplished until 1860 in Germany, where it was dubbed cocaine.

As a medicine, and particularly as a local anesthetic, cocaine's reputation slowly grew. Among its most ardent early champions was Sigmund Freud, who began using it in 1884 to treat himself, his fiancée and others for a variety of ailments. His monograph, *Über Coca,* helped popularize it as a medication.

As a stimulant, cocaine does not produce in overuse or withdrawal the same symptoms as do opium and morphine. The toxic psychosis of cocaine poisoning has no real equivalent in opiate abuse. But as the evidence of its

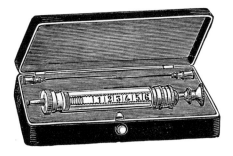

dangers became more clear, its adherents fell away, and by 1887 Freud had begun to retreat from his favorable position on cocaine, though he continued to believe it had limited medical uses.

A Triumph of Technology

Both morphine and cocaine gained significant new popularity in England thanks to a mid-nineteenth century refinement of the technology of the hypodermic syringe. Oral ingestion of the drugs tended both to delay the onset and moderate the level of their effects. But intravenous injection, as many modern-day addicts would attest, brought the psychoactive substances to the brain almost instantaneously and with much greater potency.

Watson notes in the opening of *The*

Sign of the Four, after Holmes has taken his cocaine bottle from the mantelpiece and his syringe "from its neat morocco case," his eyes "rested thoughtfully upon the sinewy forearm and wrist, all dotted and scarred with innumerable puncture-marks."

While in "The Yellow Face" Watson describes Holmes's drug use as intermittent, in *The Sign of the Four* he reports that he had witnessed Holmes go through the little ritual of injection "three times a day for many months."

Such a regimen could hardly be described as an occasional vice, even in that more tolerant era, and we would normally expect to see many more physical symptoms of addiction from Holmes. The answer may be in the fact that Watson also asks "Which is it today, morphine or cocaine?"

At the time researchers believed that because of their countervailing physical effects, cocaine could serve as a treatment for morphine addiction, and some doctors would eventually recommend morphine to relive cocaine addiction. Sherlock Holmes, whose knowledge of chemistry Dr. Watson once described as "profound," may have anticipated their efforts.

In any case Watson's disapproval apparently had some effect. In "The Adventure of the Missing Three-Quarter" Watson tells us, "For years I had gradually weaned him from that drug mania which had threatened once to check his remarkable career."

Yet Watson admits, "I was well aware that the fiend was not dead but sleeping . . . and that the sleep was a light one."

Right and below, left: Some more modern images of Sherlock Holmes.

Left (The Ritual) and above, left (from the Camden House Journal): Societies devoted to Sherlock Holmes publish a vast array of journals and newsletters.

Still, the Game's Afoot: Sherlock Holmes Societies around the World

—◁◦◦▷—

Dotted haphazardly around the globe are approximately 375 groups whose members play, sometimes with tongue in cheek, what they call the "Grand Game." Their basic tenet is that Holmes and Watson were real historical personages and that the sixty Holmes tales of the Canon are records of actual incidents as recorded by Dr. Watson. Conan Doyle was merely the literary agent.

Dame Jean Conan Doyle, daughter of Sir Arthur, once expressed her view of the readers who feel compelled to come together in a vast array of clubs and societies, saying, "My father had a great sense of humor. And the Sherlock Holmes stories made him chuckle a lot. When you realize that all this is tongue-in-cheek, and good clean fun, then you realize that this is not a collection of nutters at all. They're mostly very clever people who are having a very refreshing hobby."

For these social-minded devotees of the great detective, the most inspiring two lines in the Holmes Canon are found in "The Adventure of the Abbey Grange" in which Holmes awakens his good-natured friend early one morning with the immortal words, "Come, Watson, come. The game is afoot."

Indeed, the game—of celebrating every blade of grass trod by the lanky pipe-smoking sleuth and of leaving no canonical inconsistency unexamined—is a consuming passion that has forged bonds in the most unlikely places.

Finding Each Other

In the first third of the twentieth century, readers were content to sit alone in their armchairs for a solitary venture to Baker Street. But then, Christopher Morley appeared on the scene. An editor of the *Saturday Review of Literature* in the 1930s, the gregarious Morley had a fondness for long lunches with his literary pals with whom he frequently discussed Sherlock Holmes.

Just a month after Prohibition ended, Morley hosted a cocktail party on January 6, 1934, in honor of Holmes's birthday. Thus it was, at the Hotel Duane in New York City, that the **Baker Street Irregulars (BSI)** was born. By February of that year, the group had a constitution, albeit a frivolous and contradictory one, and in June the first formal meeting was called–for men only.

Across the Atlantic that same year, a **Sherlock Holmes Society** was founded in Great Britain. It lapsed during Europe's prewar agonies, but, in 1951, when a Sherlock Holmes exhibition attracted more than 54,000 mystery readers and memorabilia collectors during the Festival of Britain, the Society was revived and still thrives today as the **Sherlock Holmes Society of London.**

Back in the States, BSI spin-offs, called "scions," were formed across the nation, gaining momentum gradually after the war years. In 1965, frustrated that BSI remained for men only (as it would until 1991), several students from a Catholic women's college in Connecticut formed the **Adventuresses of Sherlock Holmes (ASH),** naming only one officer–the Principal Unprincipled Adventuress.

While the BSI scions and related groups popped up here and there, a Sherlockian revival swept the U.S. in 1974, generating new organizations. The revival was kindled by the publication of Nicholas Meyer's pastiche *The Seven-Per-Cent Solution* linking Holmes and Freud and of Samuel Rosenberg's *Naked Is the Best Disguise,* which examined sexual symbolism in the Canon.

The Japanese Phenomenon

The Sherlockian (or, as Europeans prefer to be called, *Holmesian*) groups

range in intent from the sublimely studious to the ridiculously playful. Nor are these groups to be found only in English-dominant nations. The world's largest organization devoted to the Baker Street Bohemian is the **Japan Sherlock Holmes Club,** with over 1,200 members. The group meets monthly in Tokyo and publishes a newsletter as well as an annual booklet and a study report. Other meetings are sponsored by its branch societies, numbering more than a dozen, located across the country.

Japan has a long tradition of devotion to things Sherlockian, though there are only a few references in the Canon to Japanese people, places or things. Sherlock Holmes hit Japan early when a translation of "The Man with the Twisted Lip" was published in the January 1894 issue of *Nipponjin.* By 1907, the first book-length translation of Holmes stories appeared.

In 1948, the **Baritsu Club,** for the purpose of studying Sherlock Holmes, was founded by twelve men in postwar occupied Tokyo, including the father of a prime minister, a premier's son, and a vice minister of finance. The world's first statue of Sherlock Holmes was erected in Japan to mark the town where the stories were first translated into Japanese. When a translation of Baring-Gould's *Sherlock Holmes of Baker Street* was published in 1977, the **Japan Sherlock Holmes Club** was founded.

The popularity of the English detective reflects Japan's fascination with Victorian society and culture that corresponded with the Meigi era in Japan. According to one news article about this phenomenon, "Under Victorian influence, the Japanese abandoned kimonos for suits, rice for bread and futons for beds."

Today, the Internet is playing its part in keeping the legend alive. In 1996, a Japanese computer club was formed, **J-Holmes.**

Auditors and Undertakers: Professionally Based Groups

Profession determines membership in a number of Sherlockian societies. There is a group for dermatologists, the **Sir James Saunders Society,** named in honor of the dermatologist with sphinxlike features Holmes consulted in "The Adventure of the Blanched Soldier." This dermatologic scion of BSI was founded in 1974 in Chicago at the annual meeting of the American Academy of Dermatology.

Though they lament the "glaring dearth of references to the insurance industry in the Canon," insurance sellers have their own Sherlockian society as well. **The Slurred Accounts of the Bribed Auditors,** founded in 1992, is named after the line in *The Valley of Fear* that claims one character's accounts were "slurred over by bribed auditors."

Stimson & Company, a Sherlockian society for funeral directors, takes its name from the only undertaker in the Canon—a character in "The Disappearance of Lady Frances Carfax." This BSI scion publishes a Gazette that examines the correlation of canonical corpses and deliberates upon those deceased. The group collects obituaries of notable Sherlockians and maintains photographic documentation of the graves of actual

Publication of Stimson & Company, a Sherlockian society for funeral directors.

people mentioned in the Canon, such as Brigham Young.

A clandestine Sherlockian society was founded in Washington, D.C., in 1971 for members of the military-industrial complex. Requests for information about this society are rarely entertained, and the membership list is classified information. Indeed, **The Bruce-Partington Planners** is so covert "that several members are not aware of its existence." Candidates for membership are examined in the fields of cryptography, identity of foreign agents, and submarine design. Not wanting a paper trail, the group has no constitution, dues, events, or reports, but they do have a motto, a sentence uttered by Sherlock Holmes himself: "We also have our diplomatic secrets."

Ramesh C. Madan, a private detective in New Delhi, is known throughout his country as the "Sherlock Holmes of India." At his own last count, this self-taught detective has saved over twenty-six innocent clients from the gallows. From childhood, his hero has been Conan Doyle's justice-seeking detective. Ramesh Madan founded the **Sherlock Holmes Society of India** in 1982. The 300 member organization meets once a month to discuss current crimes committed in Delhi and to watch Sherlock Holmes movies. Most members are police officers or military personnel who occasionally don disguises to help solve crimes. Writes Madan, "Since I am one of the leading detectives of the world, it is really fun and amusement to run a society like this. It gives lots of knowledge, thrill, sensation, chill in one's spine and, above all, satisfaction of serving the society and world community at large."

In British Columbia, William E. Ricker founded the **Binomial Theorists of Departure Bay at Nanaimo,** with other employees of the Department of Fisheries and Oceans. Ricker read his first Sherlock Holmes story at the age of twelve, in 1920, when he found a copy of *The Strand* in a stack of old magazines. There he read one installation of "The Adventure of the Speckled Band," to be continued. Fifteen years later, he bought the complete set of Holmes stories, read the conclusion, and has been a fan ever since.

Castaways and Neglected Patients: Character-Based Groups

The cohorts of Sherlock Holmes have inspired the formation of a number of societies. **The Friends of Dr. Watson,** a correspondence society founded in 1966 in Hertfordshire, England, focuses on the thirty-two doctors and thirteen references to Dr. Watson's medical knowledge and skill in the Canon. They sponsor trips to various locations of medical interest described in the Sherlock Holmes stories and publish a newsletter called *The Formulary.* The group also supports a different charity each year; in 1997 they gave a contribution to LEPTRA, which funds research and assists people afflicted with leprosy.

Doctor Watson's Neglected Patients, a Denver-based BSI scion founded in 1974, is governed by a "Medical Board" and publishes a sophisticated biannual journal, *The Medical Bulletin.*

Did Sherlock Holmes take a sabbatical in the New York City borough of Staten Island? Did he have a love affair there with photographer Alice Austen?

Members of **Watson's Tin Dispatchers** think so. Founded in 1990, the group meets monthly and takes numerous field trips, but the highlight of the year is the annual dinner with its clever menu. Between an appetizer of Five Orange Pips (fruit, cheese, and crackers) and a dessert of Illustrious Plum Pudding presented by Mrs. Hudson in Victorian garb, the Dispatchers dine on cleverly named concoctions such as Reigate Puzzle (vegetable pie), Abbey Grange Beef, Dancing Men string beans, and Jezail Rolls.

Mrs. Hudson's Cliffdwellers, organized in Cliffside Park, New Jersey, in 1976, boasts over one hundred members and meets twice a year. Devoted to having fun, the group engages in sing-alongs and quiz competitions for which the prize might be a picture of Irene Adler as an infant, bare on a bear rug.

The Occupants of the Empty House, a Southern Illinois group in existence for over twenty years, publishes *The Camden House Journal.* The group's president wears the title, "Master of the House," while the vice president is known as "The Waxen Image." The group's motto is "the prime detective is the prime directive."

Dr. Watson and Mrs. Hudson are not the only Sherlock Holmes confederates to inspire the founding of an organization. The Iowa City-based **Younger Stamfords,** named for the crucial person who introduced Watson and Holmes in *A Study in Scarlet,* was founded by Dr. Richard M. Caplan, who, in 1988, ran an announcement in a local newspaper advertising for "red-headed men." According to Caplan,

I thought that any Sherlockians who might be attracted to come to an initial meeting would of course recognize the circumstances. I received six telephone calls in response; five of them were indeed red-headed persons. None of them had read any Sherlock Holmes but were either curious about my ad or thought that I was running some sort of dating service. Fortunately, however, I had occasion to speak with a reporter from that newspaper about the ad. He thought the circumstances would make an interesting story, so he prepared a little feature article about me and Sherlockian interests. That produced a veritable flood of interest and we had twenty-eight people attend that first meeting.

Some groups have named themselves after people on the fringe of the Canon. The Minneapolis-based **Lady Frances Carfax Society** was founded in the early 1980s by an unmarried woman who liked the idea, as proclaimed by Holmes in the story about the Lady's disappearance, that "one of the most dangerous classes in the world is the drifting and friendless woman . . . She is a stray chicken in a world of foxes."

The **Spence Munros** of Nova Scotia, founded in 1981, named themselves after the former employer of Violet Hunter in "The Adventure of the Copper Beeches," who eventually moved to Nova Scotia.

In Belfast, Northern Ireland, a group called the **Crew of the SS *May Day*** meets once a month. They take their name from "The Adventure of the Cardboard Box" in which Jim Browner, steward of the SS *May Day*, travels from Liverpool to Belfast and mails the infamous package containing human ears.

In Lisbon, Portugal, a Sherlockian group called **The Norah Creina Castaways** honors the only reference to Portugal in the Canon. In "The Adventure of the Resident Patient" the *Norah Creina* is shipwrecked and all hands are lost on the Portuguese coast. Holmesian scholar and pastiche author, Joel Lima, the group's founder, maintains a regular Sherlockian department in the **Associaçao Policiária Portuguesa,** Portugal's only detection club.

At least two groups share the name **The Priory Scholars.** One, founded in New York City in 1953, was originally a repertory group that performed new Sherlock Holmes radio shows for a Fordham University station. This group still meets four to six times a year and has approximately 150 members. At one meeting in 1996, two of the members were married by a lawyer who had represented the Conan Doyle estate.

The Priory Scholars of Leicester, England, takes "school trips" to Holmesian locations in and around London. They have visited Dartmoor, Norfolk, and the Baker Street set of the Granada TV Studios in Manchester. They also publish a quarterly newsletter, *The School Report.*

One group based in Peoria, Illinois, named itself after a Victorian mode of transportation featured in *The Hound of the Baskervilles*–**The Hansoms of John Clayton.** In the most poplar Sherlock Holmes novel, John Clayton drove the disguised Stapleton about London in a hansom, a two-wheeled covered carriage drawn by a single horse. The group,

founded in 1977 by science fiction author Philip Jose Farmer, publishes a monthly newsletter *Plugs & Dottles,* which takes its name from a descriptive line in "The Adventure of the Engineer's Thumb":

> and smoking his before-breakfast pipe, which was composed of all the plugs and dottles left of his smokes of the day before, all carefully dried and collected on the corner mantel-piece.

The group opens its six yearly meetings with a responsive reading of the *"Clayton Ritual."*

> What was his name:
> John Clayton.
>
> Where did he live?
> No. 3, Turpey Street, the Borough.
>
> What did he do?
> He drove a hansom cab.
>
> And what was its number?
> 2704.
>
> Whence came the cab?
> Out of Shipley's Yard, near Waterloo Station.
>
> When was his famous ride?
> September 26, 1888.
>
> And who was his infamous fare?
> Rodger Baskerville, alias Stapleton, alias Vandeleur.

Every meeting ends with a reading of Vincent Starrett's poem "221B" which affirms, "Here dwell together still two men of note, who never lived and so can never die."

Logo of the Scotland Yarders.

The Scotland Yarders have been meeting in the Chicago area since 1988. The members, now numbering more than sixty, include doctors, lawyers, computer programmers, librarians, teachers, a comic book artist, and one police officer who collects Victorian police memorabilia. The group publishes *The Police Gazette,* which always includes beneath the masthead this quote by Holmes from "His Last Bow": "Scotland Yard feels lonely without me."

Donning the Deerstalkers: Action-Oriented Groups

Sometimes a Sherlockian group will name itself after a story title. This is true of **The Six Napoleons** of Baltimore,

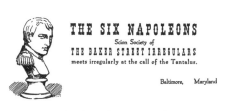

Letterhead of The Six Napoleons.

Maryland, founded in 1946 by six men. For a number of years, every candidate for membership was required to visit the Baltimore grave of Edgar Allan Poe, who is generally considered the father of the detective story. While this tradition has died out, the group, now numbering almost fifty, still sponsors an annual symposium called "A Saturday with Sherlock Holmes," an event held at a public library and featuring lectures, films, and Sherlockian games and quizzes.

The Noble and Most Singular Order of the Blue Carbuncle, which began as a literature class at a local college, has been meeting monthly in Portland, Oregon, for over twenty-five years. Every May the group celebrates "Reichenbach Day" in honor of the battle between Holmes and Moriarty. The group's members dress in Victorian mourning clothing and, at noon are led by a bagpiper up a path to Multnomah Falls for a special ceremony. On Labor Day weekend, the group sponsors a four-day retreat complete with high teas, an evening of Victorian elegance, presentations, a talent show, and other fun events. Three times a year they stage original mystery plays, often raising funds for a good cause. After one fund-raiser, they purchased a police dog for the city.

The Sydney Passengers is an Australian society founded in 1985 that takes its name from the survivors of a mutiny at sea who were picked up by a passenger ship bound for Sydney in "The Adventure of the 'Gloria Scott.'" This group boasts of the time, in January 1989, when they dressed in Victorian costume and picketed the

Logo of The Sydney Passengers.

first screening of *Without a Clue* because the movie portrayed Holmes as a drunken lecherous bungler. Another favorite anecdote of the group concerns a young woman who was encouraged by her mother to attend a meeting, but who feared the group would be full of eccentrics. When she finally yielded, she not only became committed to the Sydney Passengers, but fell in love with one of them. The mystery-loving couple were eventually married at one of the meetings.

The Singular Society of the Baker Street Dozen, a Canadian group established in Calgary, Alberta, in 1987, enjoys reading Conan Doyle's adventures with an eye to counting the remarkable number of times the word "singular" appears. In what was arguably their most exciting meeting, the club was celebrating the master detective's birthday one January 6th at the home of Stephen Forrester and his pregnant wife Irena, when Irena's water broke and she was rushed to the hospital where she gave birth to a *singular* bundle of joy.

L'Hotel de Dulong is a Holmesian group in Lyon, France, named after the hotel where Watson found Holmes lying ill in "The Adventure of the Reigate Squires." It publishes *Le Registre* and aims to retranslate the Holmes stories in French, correcting previous inaccuracies. Sylvain Policard, alias Le Directeur Dulong Père, accompanied more than sixty representatives of various French Holmes societies on a pilgrimage to Reichenbach, Switzerland, in May 1995. According to his notes, the devotees assembled in a Parisian location, in Victorian costume, looking for the lost luggage of Watson and Holmes. They then traveled by train to Meiringen, Switzerland, where they stayed in a picturesque chalet and "spent many hours in Holmesian discussions upon glasses of beer at the bar." After taking in the magnificent mountain landscapes and enjoying a cocktail party organized by local officials in the Meiringen Sherlock Holmes Museum, the group headed for Reichenbach Falls, the infamous site of Holmes' death struggle with Moriarty. In personal correspondence, Policard described the venture.

> The last day was devoted to the Reichenbach ascent, for ascent is the word. You have pretty little mountain pastures and quite steep paths. No wonder the Professor did a false step, since the closer you get to the Falls, the more soaked you become because of the spray, and so becomes the soil all around the hole. Even if a railing runs between you and the abyss at the presumed spot of the last fight, it would be no hard job to fall in the rumbling overflow of those frightening alpine waterfalls. We threw bunches of flowers from the footbridge which spans the top of the Falls and filled up bottles with freezing water from the very sides of Reichenbach.

Of Like Minds:
Special Interest Groups

Members of **Holmesian Studies SIG,** a "special interest group" of **American MENSA** (whose requirement for membership is a high IQ), prefer armchair adventures to traipsing up spray-drenched mountain paths. Their newsletter, *The Norbury Chronicle,* features an array of secret codes to decipher and puzzles to solve. The newsletter's name is an allusion to a moment of Holmesian humility when, chagrined by his failure in the Grant Munro case in "The Adventure of the Yellow Face," he said, "Watson, if it should ever strike you that I am getting a little over-confident in my powers, or giving less pains to a case than it deserves, kindly whisper 'Norbury' in my ear, and I shall be infinitely obliged to you." One interesting anecdote from this group, the only bad check they ever received was from a MENSA member named Moriarty.

The Olde Pips of Florida, an organization designed for seniors wintering near Tampa, gather to share their love of the stories.

Martha Hudson's Cronies, a "cache of wily sleuths . . . as ageless as their spirits of adventure," meets monthly around a sitting room at the Nicollet Care Center in Minneapolis. Fierce in their devotion to Holmes and to their independence, they read the adventures, pose questions, and debate various theories. One of the group's associates, who can remember the past in vivid detail but who sometimes cannot recall where her room is located, taped a picture of Sherlock Holmes on her door and hasn't lost her way since.

Billing itself as "the only Sherlockian service organization," **The American Firm** raises funds to purchase large-type print editions of Sherlock Holmes books for nursing homes. The owner of a real estate franchise founded the group of philanthropic Sherlockians because he had personal experiences with nursing homes and knew that books could help pass the time. Through its "Resident Patient Fund," the group gave more than fifty books in just the first two years.

Logo of The American Firm.

Occasionally societies for the younger set emerge, usually from the classroom. Such was the case in 1987, when Mohamad Bazzi, a seventh grade student in the New York City borough of Queens, was turned on to Holmes by a classmate. Once bitten by the Baker Street bug, there was no stopping the teen. He and his friends found a teacher willing to run a Sherlock Holmes discussion group after school, and, in 1989, **The Young Sherlockians of New York** was officially established as a citywide organization for students in public schools. The group was greatly encouraged by adult Sherlockian luminaries, including John Bennett Shaw, Thomas Stix, Jr., Peter Blau, and Tom Utecht.

This was just the beginning. Bazzi

and his friend Andrew Ronan borrowed money from the school principal to produce two magazines, *221-B* and *The Sherlockian Tabloid,* for which they wrote original stories and essays. The enterprising Bazzi then sought and received funding from the Queens Council on the Arts to launch a drama program, *The Sherlockian Theater,* through which the students staged three plays for the public.

Billing themselves as a "a traveling barter-shop quartet," **the Midwest Scion of the Four** was founded in Peoria, Illinois, in 1987 by four active memorabilia collectors from Missouri and Illinois who kept running into each other at various Sherlockian society symposiums. They decided to hold a scion meeting whenever the four were together, established "bye-laws," and composed a scion song which includes these words:

> *With fast cars and Canons, the scion it roams,*
> *Wherever they travel, they travel with Holmes.*

According to Joe Eckrich, who is also active in **The Parallel Case of St. Louis,** a group founded in 1988, The Midwest Scion of the Four was founded "wholly in fun, which is really the only reason to found a group dedicated to Sherlock Holmes, although some groups do take things a little bit more serious."

The Scholarly Societies

One of the organizations that prides itself on "taking things a little bit more serious" can be found in Spain: **The**

Masthead of "The Parallelogram," a publication of The Parallel Case of St. Louis.

Amateur Mendicant Society of Madrid. It is named for an organization investigated by Holmes in 1887 as described in "The Five Orange Pips," which ran a luxurious club in the vault of a furniture warehouse. The Mendicants are solely a scholarly group; Victorian dress occasions, amateur theatrics, the "fanatical collection of allegedly Holmesian items" are all discouraged. Their studies are canonical and pastiches are "entirely out of the question." Each member is expected to present at least one scholarly contribution per year. Mendicant means beggar, so it is fitting that the group's annual celebration of Holmes is called "The Day of the Beggar."

The Franco-Midland Hardware Company (known as **FMHC** or **The Company**) is an international Sherlock Holmes Study Group. Based in the United Kingdom, it claims to be one of the largest and most active Holmesian societies in the world, with members from more than forty countries involved in correspondence study courses. The Company typically releases more than fourteen publications a year of various styles and sizes and organizes numerous events, such as a dinner aboard a steam train at the site of one of the canonical adventures and an eight-day expedition to Reichenbach in Switzerland. They have also erected a plaque at Conan Doyle's home in Hindhead. The official motto of the group is, "The game is still afoot," and the unofficial motto is, "Do not be a dog in the nighttime."

The Arthur Conan Doyle Study Group, a branch office of The Company, was formed in 1996 in response to an expressed need for Holmesians to learn more about the Scottish-born author. They publish a newsletter, *The Cerebral Tentacle.*

At least two societies exist for the purpose of studying one story each. **The Baskerville Hounds,** not surprisingly, is devoted to the study of *The Hound of the Baskervilles.* Philip Weller, its founder and organizer, is known as the Master of the Hounds, with Jane Weller, the overworked secretary, called The Kennel Maid. Based in Hampshire, England, the group publishes a journal, *The Hound,* and a newsletter, *Kennel News,* and organizes at least four meetings a year, most of these being full weekend events on Dartmoor. The Pack Meet is a weekend event held close to the crucial October 16th events outlined in the story.

Another single-story focused group is **STUD,** an invitation-only Sherlockian society and its membership is honorary, based on canonical accomplishment and knowledge. The group occasionally gives financial support to worthwhile Sherlockian causes like the Holmes collection at the Chicago Public Library. Founded in 1991, its sole purpose is to provide a forum for the exclusive study of Conan Doyle's first Sherlock Holmes story, *A Study in Scarlet.* It is traditionally called to order by the "STUDmaster" on or about March 3rd or 4th, to correspond with the timing of the date central to the adventure. The group also sponsors a Sherlockian automobile race known as the Rache Road Rally, "Rache" being the German word for revenge, which was scrawled in blood upon the wall at Lauriston Gardens.

The Sherlock Holmes Society of London was formed in 1951 for the purpose of studying the life and work of Sherlock Holmes and Dr. Watson and of their creator, Sir Arthur Conan Doyle. It is expressly a literary society, not a "fan

"The Cerebral Tentacle," the newsletter of The Arthur Conan Doyle Study Group.

The Case of the Theological Implications

The Protective Order of the Persian Slipper, founded in 1981, bills itself as "an evangelical organization devoted to spreading the gospel of Sherlockiana to the great unread of Madison, Georgia." Its Chief Tobacconist hosts a gathering once a year where fifty people are invited to "hear the Word." Many, it is proudly reported, are converted and go forth to study the saga of Holmes and Watson.

While the Protective Order is candid in its toying with religious language, theological terminology is frequently used among Sherlockians. Holmes is commonly referred to as "The Master." The collected stories about his cases are called "The Sacred Writings" or "The Canon." The post-Doylian writings about Holmes are called "The Apocrypha," another term borrowed from the vocabulary of organized religion.

Holmes's birthday is commemorated by most Sherlockians on January 6th, a date suggested by BSI founder Christopher Morley, in part because, twice, Holmes quotes Shakespeare's play *Twelfth Night.* January 6, the twelfth day after Christmas, is celebrated by many Christians as Epiphany, the observance of the arrival of the three kings who traveled from the Orient to kneel before the holy child.

Holmes does battle with the forces of death (the Latin word *mortuarius* means "of the dead" and *mori* means "to die") and, in wrestling Moriarty, is willing to give his life for the salvation of–in this case, England.

Both the "death" of Sherlock Holmes and his return, three years later, occur in the spring, not unlike another death and resurrection ritual.

club" and boasts more than one thousand members, of whom about one-third are overseas.

In 1994 the Society sponsored a ten-day London festival called "Back to Baker Street" to celebrate the centenary of Holmes's return after the Great Hiatus. The events included a symposium held at Scotland Yard on Holmes and the police, and a mock inquest, based on incidents in "The Adventure of the Empty House." The highlight of the festival was the unveiling of a plaque at No. 2, Upper Wimpole Street, by Sir Arthur's daughter, Dame Jean Conan Doyle, commemorating the house where her father wrote many of the early Sherlock Holmes stories.

Baker Street and Beyond: Geographically Based Groups

Geography often determines the focus of the Sherlockian society and gives a group its name. **The Montague Street Lodgers,** founded in 1986, meets quarterly in various restaurants along trendy Montague Street in Brooklyn; Holmes had rooms on London's Montague Street when he first began his practice as a consulting detective.

Lamenting that Sherlock Holmes is not very popular in Belgium, the **221Bees** nevertheless persist with two enthusiastic members, a husband and wife team known as the Queen Bee and the Worker Bee. Their motto is "To bee or not to bee," and their goal is to fill in a blank spot on the Holmesian map. Passionate in their devotion to the master detective, the couple has traced the footsteps of Conan Doyle in Great Britain and hosted a Sherlockian tour of Belgium.

Some "serious Sherlockians" in Texas formed the **Diogenes Club of Dallas,** taking their name from a fraternal group mentioned in "The Adventure of the Greek Interpreter," which Holmes called "the queerest club in London" for "the most unsociable and unclubable men in town."

Another group named for a canonical meeting place is the Chicago-based **Criterion Bar Association,** named after the elegant restaurant bar located in Regent Circus, Piccadilly where Watson met young Stamford in *A Study in Scarlet*. The members claim that, one year, at their January birthday observance, Mr. Holmes himself was a guest of honor.

Salt Lake City, Utah, headquarters of the Mormon Church, hosts the **Avenging Angels,** named after the secret society of Mormons mentioned in *A Study in Scarlet*. The modern society was founded in 1991 by Ronald De Waal, whose Holmesian bibliography is considered an essential resource to students of the Canon.

An Irish Secret Society at Buffalo offers companionship to Holmes enthusiasts in western New York State. Named after a group mentioned in "His Last Bow," it evolved from a 1976 adult-education course on Sherlock Holmes.

Just across Lake Ontario, the **Bootmakers of Toronto** boast some 350 members ranging in age from eight to eighty, and is thought to be the biggest regularly meeting society in North America. This Canadian society's name comes from a reference in *The Hound of the Baskervilles*; when Holmes

Logo of the Bootmakers of Toronto.

sinks to his waist in mud on the moor to pull out Sir Henry's missing black boot, he finds printed on the leather the name of the bootmaker, *"Meyers, Toronto."*

The Sherlock Holmes Society of Australia was founded in 1978 in Adelaide, a city visited by Sir Arthur Conan Doyle and his family in 1920. A commemorative plaque now marks the site of the hotel in which the Doyle family stayed.

The **Northern Musgraves Sherlock Holmes Society,** formed in 1987 to provide a forum in the North of England, today has an international membership. It boasts a logo designed by the late Peter Cushing, an actor who portrayed Holmes in the 1959 film version of *The Hound of the Baskervilles.* The group takes its name from "The Adventure of the Musgrave Ritual," a mystery solved by Holmes before he met Watson.

The Poor Folk upon the Moors is a Sherlock Holmes Society in England that takes its name from a statement by a character in *The Hound of the Baskervilles,* who says, "My brother is very anxious to have the Hall inhabited, for he thinks it is for the good of the poor folk upon the moor." The eighty-member group publishes *The Torr,* a biannual journal of Holmesian studies and sponsors a Dartmoor Walk once a year in good weather, as well as an annual feast of Christmas goose, with the merry diners wearing Victorian costume.

Three times a year, the sixty-plus members from the Tampa/St. Petersburg area meet for lunch not far from Holmes Beach, a stretch of sunshine-drenched sand along the Gulf of Mexico. They call their group the **Pleasant Places of Florida,** after the spirit with

Biannual publication of an English Holmesian Society.

Quarterly publication of The Baskerville Hall Club of Sweden.

which Sherlock Holmes spoke in "The Five Orange Pips" when he said, "Men at this time of life do not change all their habits, and exchange willingly the charming climate of Florida for the lonely life of an English provincial town."

The **Regina Irregulars** of Saskatchewan sometimes travel 250 miles to join with members of **The Casebook of Saskatoon,** Canada's second oldest Sherlockian society. Severe winter weather often limits their activities.

Isolating conditions are not limited to cold climes nor do they stifle the committed devotees of Sherlock Holmes. When Candace Drimmer was living in Paraguay, she didn't let the numerous power outages stop her reading. Huddled over a volume of Baring-Gould's *Annotated Sherlock Holmes* with only a kerosene lamp to illumine the book, she was inspired by the parallel between the gas-lit world of Holmes in nineteenth century London and her own experience. She subsequently founded **The Solitary Sherlockian,** based on the theory "that it is the nature of both the Master and we, his students, to be solitary individuals. For that reason, the activities of our scion are strictly limited to non-communal ventures and membership is limited to one solitary person per country."

Global Adventurers

There are Sherlockians who would hoard the adventures, lay claim to the "game," declare themselves the rightful heirs of the master detective's mystery, and erect barriers to keep the riffraff out. Most true devotees, however, are extravagant in their generosity, sincerely welcoming new converts.

When George Vanderburgh was called out of retirement to travel as a medical officer with the Canadian forces serving with the United Nations Forces in Somalia, all he could think was that there was no known Sherlock Holmes Society in Africa nor Kiswahili translations of the stories. Even before his jet lag had abated, he was investigating available translations of works by Conan Doyle. Soon after, he set out to trace Conan Doyle's footsteps in Nairobi and to commission Swahili translations of *The Hound of the Baskervilles* and "The Adventure of the Speckled Band." By the time he returned to Canada, he had founded **Dr. Sterndale's Lion Hunters.**

Sherlock Holmes around the World (S.H.A.W.) calls itself "a foreign language Sherlockian Society." It publishes a periodical expressly for collectors of foreign editions of the Canon

Logo of S.H.A.W–a foreign-language society.

and celebrates the world's first consulting detective as an international phenomenon. According to one researcher, the Sherlock Holmes stories have been translated into sixty-two languages, sixty-three if you count Pig-Latin. In languages as diverse as Czech and Yiddish, and in forms as distinct as Braille and Gregg shorthand, well over 1,400 editions of the Sherlock Holmes stories have appeared in print.

The world is literally at the fingertips of Holmes devotees with the development of the most recent resource–the Internet. Holmes is mentioned on thousands of pages of the World Wide Web, and dozens of sites kept by individuals and groups are devoted exclusively to Holmes, the Canon and its characters and situations. They include such cleverly-named sites as "Sherlocktron," "Mrs. Hudson's Home Page," "Jabez Wilson's Basement," "Gaslight on the Web," and the "Web-Headed League."

The sites range widely in quality, but a number have the text of the Holmes stories and extensive information on Holmes in the movies and on television, including pictures of the actors who have played major roles. Others offer Holmes "chat" and the opportunity to purchase memorabilia.

The Adventure of the Reigate Squires

First Publication:

The Strand Magazine, June 1893

Principal Predicament:

With Holmes in a state of nervous prostration, Watson arranges a little holiday near Reigate in Surrey. No sooner have the good doctor and the depressed bachelor arrived on the scene than they learn of a recent, unsolved mystery. Someone has ransacked the library of Old Acton, a local magnate. Though the thieves turned the place upside down, they took nothing more than one book, two candlesticks, a letter-weight, a barometer, and a ball of twine. This news almost puts the gleam back in Holmes's eye, but his mood definitely improves when it is announced, over next morning's breakfast, that the Cunningham's coachman, William, has been shot through the heart and killed in connection with what appears to be another burglary. The police confer with the esteemed detective from London and show Holmes a piece of torn paper William was clutching when he died. With a glance at the handwriting on the paper, Holmes exclaims, "These are much deeper waters than I had thought." The color is back in his cheeks.

Notable Features:

(1) Holmes's behavior in this adventure is at times disturbing. He appears to writhe in agony in the grip of a seizure. Later, Watson is pained when Holmes apparently makes an error that needs to be corrected by the elderly Cunningham. Still later in the story, Holmes knocks over a dish of oranges and a carafe of water and then blames Watson, most unfairly. (2) In American publications this story is generally titled "The Reigate Puzzle."

Quotable Quote:

Holmes: "It has always been my habit to hide none of my methods, either from my friend Watson or from anyone who might take an intelligent interest in them."

The Adventure of the Crooked Man

First Publication:

The Strand Magazine, July 1893

Principal Predicament:

The detecting duo travels to Aldershot to investigate what Holmes gleefully calls "one of the strangest cases which ever perplexed a man's brain." It seems that the highly regarded Colonel James Barclay is dead and may have been murdered; his beloved wife is the prime suspect. The two had been arguing in the morning room, and the servants had heard Mrs. Barclay's bitter voice cry out, "You coward!" and then, "I will never so much as breathe the same air with you again." A series of dreadful cries brought the coachman who, finding the door barred, ran out to the lawn and entered the room through the long French windows. There he found his master stone dead in a pool of blood beside a club of carved wood and Mrs. Barclay passed out on the couch nearby. Investigating the case, Holmes finds two sets of footprints on the lawn, one set belonging to an unidentified animal. A Miss Morrison confesses that she had accompanied Mrs. Barclay to a charity meeting at the Wall Street Mission and, while walking home, had encountered a deformed man with a dark and fearsome face who

cried out, "My God, it's Nancy!" Mrs. Barclay had turned as white as death, but stopped to speak to the wretch, whom she called by name. Shortly after her return to the house, Mrs. Barclay had argued loudly with her husband who was never seen alive again. One last thing: though her husband's name was James and the deformed wretch's name was Henry, Mrs. Barclay was heard to cry out the name "David!" twice in the fatal argument. Too bad Holmes's biblical knowledge is, as he confesses to Watson, "a trifle rusty."

"He stopped and screamed out in a dreadful voice, 'My God, it's Nancy!' Mrs. Barclay turned as white as death, and would have fallen down had the dreadful-looking creature not caught hold of her." Sidney Paget 1893

The Adventure of the Resident Patient

First Publication:

The Strand Magazine, August 1893

Principal Predicament:

Dr. Percy Trevelyan is perplexed by an odd chain of events. He had established a practice in the home of his wealthy benefactor, Mr. Blessington. Not long ago, a frail, elderly man identified as a Russian nobleman suffering from cataleptic attacks had arrived at the doctor's office, accompanied by his handsome son. When the nobleman had a seizure, the doctor dashed off to his laboratory for a bottle of medicine (nitrite of amyl). When he returned five minutes later, both father and son were gone. To the doctor's amazement, the duo appeared the next evening, their explanations and sheepish apologies in order. This time, they engaged in a half-hour consultation with the doctor and left after cordial good-byes. But no sooner had they left than Mr. Blessington burst into the office in a panic. "Who has been in my room?" he cried. Holmes and Watson are then consulted, but the very next morning, Blessington is found hanging in his bedroom, clad in his nightdress.

Fleet Street, where Holmes and Watson strolled about together for three hours, watching the ever-changing kaleidoscope of life as it ebbed and flowed. Credit: Radio Times Hulton Picture Library

The Adventure of the Greek Interpreter

First Publication:

The Strand Magazine, September 1893

Principal Predicament:

On Monday night Mr. Melas, Mycroft Holmes's neighbor, found himself in a carriage with a menacing man carrying a bludgeon. He was driven about for two hours. At the end of his journey he was ushered into a richly furnished room to assist in the attempt to force a Greek gentleman, who was emaciated and gagged, to sign some documents. Under the noses of the kidnappers, the interpreter cleverly managed to elicit information about the prisoner, when, suddenly, a door opened and a tall, black-haired woman entered the room. She cried out, "Oh, my God, it is Paul!" The starved victim burst through the gag to cry out, "Sophy! Sophy!" Moments later, the bewildered Mr. Melas was placed in the coach and driven to Wandsworth Common. He tells Watson and the Holmes brothers that he'd like to be of help to the unhappy man being held prisoner.

Notable Feature:

In this story we learn about Holmes's family background and meet his elder brother, Mycroft.

ODDITIES AND DISCREPANCIES:

In *A Study in Scarlet,* Holmes insisted that the study of astronomy was useless, but in this story Holmes is able to discuss "the change in the obliquity of the ecliptic."

"There are many men in London . . . who, some from shyness, some from misanthropy have no wish for the company of their fellows. Yet they are not averse to comfortable chairs and the latest periodicals. It is for the convenience of these that the Diogenes Club was started . . ."

Great Matters of State

＊＊＊

Even casual students of the Canon are aware that Sherlock Holmes's brother Mycroft played a key role in the councils of Her Majesty's government.

According to Sherlock, "Again and again his word has decided the national policy . . . occasionally he *is* the British government." He describes his brother as "a subordinate, has no ambitions of any kind, will receive neither honor nor title, but remains the most indispensable man in the country."

But we know from many passing references and veiled allusions in the Canon, along with several stories, that during his long career Sherlock himself played an important role in matters of international consequence.

Is it likely that the Pope would have asked him to investigate the sudden death of Cardinal Tosca (mentioned in "The Adventure of Black Peter") if the demise of that Prince of the Church were merely a private matter?

Holmes's client in "A Scandal in Bohemia" laid his problem before the great detective with the statement that the affair "may have an influence on European history" (though his agitation was such that we may forgive a bit of exaggeration). Holmes's services to the royal families of Holland and Scandinavia (mentioned in "A Scandal in Bohemia" and "The Adventure of the Noble Bachelor" respectively) along with his commission on behalf of the Sultan of Turkey ("The Adventure of the Blanched Soldier"), may have been other than diplomatic. But if his missions had failed, would there not have been diplomatic repercussions?

Though we do not know the details, we know from Holmes's own lips that it was he who saved the Count von und zu Grafenstein from death at the hands of the Nihilist Klopman ("His Last Bow"), and it was a matter of public record that he had been engaged in 1891 in the service of the French Republic on what Watson refers to as "a matter of supreme importance" ("The Final Problem"), and that he had accepted elevation to the Legion of Honor from a grateful France.

In addition, his skills were put to use by a number of present and former lead-

Pope Leo XIII called on Holmes for help.

ing members of the British government in their private capacities. The Duke of Holdernesse, a former Lord of the Admiralty and Cabinet member, consulted him in "The Adventure of the Priory School." It was "one of the highest, noblest, most exalted names in England" on whose ultimate behalf Holmes recovered the jewels of "The Adventure of the Beryl Coronet." And we can only speculate on the identity of the officeholder, along with the nature of the problem, in the famous but unchronicled case of "the politician, the lighthouse and the trained cormorant" (mentioned in "The Adventure of the Veiled Lodger").

But we do have the details of four cases–"The Naval Treaty," "The Adventure of the Second Stain," "The Adventure of the Bruce-Partington Plans," and "His Last Bow"–in which Holmes's role in European political history was clear-cut and potentially decisive.

England and Europe

Through the period of the Holmes stories, England stood in peculiar relation to her neighbors on the Continent. Far smaller, and geographically isolated, only her industrial might and worldwide empire made her a significant player in Continental affairs.

For hundreds of years after the Norman invasion of 1066, English kings retained feudal ties and obligations to France, not to mention titles to large tracts of French countryside. It was to reinforce those claims that English kings like Henry V went campaigning into France. But by the time of Queen

Elizabeth in the seventeenth century the sea had become the battleground of English interests.

England eventually relinquished most of her territorial interests on the Continent, and as the empire grew the English came to believe that her security depended on maintaining a balance of power among the great European states, preventing one from growing so large that it could threaten English sovereignty.

Queen Victoria.

While in the twentieth century England and France have been allies in two world wars, in Holmes's time England's most recent Continental enemy had been France, and its most recent European ally had been Prussia. It was English and Prussian troops together who had defeated Napoleon at Waterloo and brought about nearly a century–with notable interruptions–of peace among the Great Powers.

In addition, England's ruling house was the Saxe-Coburg-Gotha, originally a German line whose name was changed to Windsor only after the turn of the present century; the German Kaiser was a grandson of Queen Victoria; and there was a wealth of commercial and personal ties between England and the recently united Germany (it was, after all, to perfect his German that young Conan Doyle was sent to school in Austria).

Nevertheless, it was becoming more and more clear that while France had once been the destabilizing influence, a united, industrializing, and ambitious Germany was posing a greater and greater threat to the balance of European power.

The Secret Covenant

The subject of "The Naval Treaty" is an agreement designed to help insure that balance. It "defined the position of Great Britain toward the Triple Alliance" (then Germany, Austria-Hungary, and Italy), and "foreshadowed the policy this country would pursue in the event of the French fleet gaining a complete ascendancy over the Italian in the Mediterranean." (Such was the remaining importance of French power and diplomacy in the late nineteenth century that the treaty between Great Britain and Italy was written neither in English nor Italian but in French.)

Lord Holdhurst, the British cabinet member to whom Holmes goes to discuss the missing treaty, foresees "very grave results indeed" should the treaty find its way into the hands of the French or Russian ambassadors. And it is partially to prevent the potential release of the details that Holmes allows the thief to flee unencumbered once the treaty itself is recovered, reasoning that Lord Holdhurst and others concerned "would

very much rather that the affair never got as far as a police-court."

"So Provocative a Character. . . . "

In "The Adventure of the Second Stain" another state document is missing, this a piece of correspondence "from a certain foreign potentate." "Of so provocative a character" are this sovereign's writings, according to the Prime Minister and Secretary of State for European Affairs, who have come to Baker Street to seek Holmes's guidance, that "within a week of the publication of that letter this country would be involved in a great war."

"The whole of Europe is an armed camp," the Prime Minister tells Holmes. "There is a double league which makes a fair balance of military power. Great Britain holds the scales. If Britain were driven into war with one confederacy, it would assure the supremacy of the other confederacy."

"It is then the interest of the enemies of this potentate to secure and publish this letter, so as to make a breach between his country and ours?" asks Holmes.

"Yes, sir," replies the statesman.

Holmes's discovery of the missing document before it could be conveyed to the Continent delighted the Premier, who made no objection when Holmes preferred not to relate the details of its recovery, saying only that "We also have our diplomatic secrets."

"The Most Jealously Guarded of All Government Secrets. . . . "

The key to England's political and

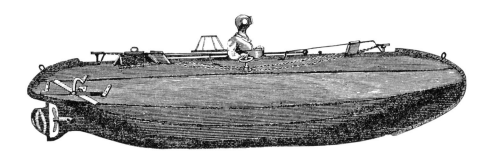

economic success lay in its command of the sea, for it was by the sea that she ruled and traded with her colonies, and by the sea that food and raw materials came to her. The German fleet grew in the late nineteenth century, and England and Germany competed to build ever larger dreadnoughts and more powerful battleships that at the time represented the cutting edge of military technology.

But posing an even greater potential threat to England's naval supremacy was the invention of a militarily capable submarine, and in "The Adventure of the Bruce-Partington Plans" the designs for such a vessel have been stolen.

"You may take it from me that naval warfare becomes impossible within the radius of a Bruce-Partington's operation," Mycroft Holmes told his brother, referring to the submarine by the names of its designers. "In all your career you have never had so great a chance of serving your country."

Before the matter was concluded with British interests intact, Holmes was given to believe that not only the Cabinet awaited his report, but that "urgent representations have arrived from the very highest quarter" about his progress. It was apparently from that quarter that Holmes received a "remarkably fine emerald tie pin" that he told Watson was "a present from a certain gracious lady in whose interests he had once been fortunate enough to carry out a small commission."

His Last Bow

We may presume in "The Adventure of the Mazarin Stone" that, since the Prime Minister brought with him to Baker Street only the Home Secretary, the issue at hand–the loss of the Crown diamond–was of purely domestic consequences. But it was another matter indeed in ""His Last Bow" when the shadow of war hung above all of England, including Holmes's retirement retreat upon the Sussex Downs.

"The Foreign Minister alone I could have withstood, but when the Premier also deigned to visit my humble roof . . ." Holmes tells Watson. The story is set in August 1914, just prior to the outbreak of World War I. Holmes, plucked from his beekeeping, has spent a considerable period in the United States and Ireland creating a character named Altamont, an Irish-American filled with hatred for Britain and a paid spy in the employ of the German Von Bork.

Only as Von Bork prepares to leave England with a trunkload of intelligence, including vital naval signals, does Holmes reveal himself as a British operative who has masterminded the capture of Von Bork's other agents, in addition to providing a trove of misleading information to Von Bork and his government.

"Your admiral may find the new guns rather larger than he expects, and the cruisers perhaps a trifle faster," Holmes tells Von Bork.

As the story ends he feels an east wind coming and says to Watson, "such a wind as never blew on England yet. It will be cold and bitter, Watson, and a good many of us may wither before its blast."

The wind was indeed to be fierce, and among its victims was Conan Doyle's son and younger brother.

They, however, were but two of many. In "The Adventure of the Second Stain" the Premier and the Secretary of State tell Holmes that war could well be the result of the public release of the missing document, telling him that "the lives of a hundred thousand men" hang in the balance.

That number was far too optimistic. By the time of World War I, any of the major combatants could expect to lose that many men in a single battle. In the

Sherlockian researcher William S. Baring-Gould conjectured that the Prime Minister who visited the Baker Street flat in "The Adventure of the Mazarin Stone" was Arthur James Balfour.

Battle of the Somme the British took 60,000 casualties in the first day alone. Conan Doyle's son Kingsley was wounded but survived. His constitution weakened, he died of influenza shortly before the war ended in 1918. Conan Doyle's brother Innes, who had fought the war for four years, died in similar circumstances a few months later.

PUZZLER

Who's Who and What Did They Do?

Can you find the description for each of the following?

Mycroft, Wiggins, Irene Adler, Violet Smith, Mary Morstan, Lestrade, Mrs. Hudson, Stamford, Moriarty, Billy, Sebastian Moran, Milverton, Selden, Fred Porlock, Jabez Wilson

_____ 1. A young but very wise and tactful page at Baker Street.

_____ 2. The surgeon's assistant at Bart's who introduced Watson and Holmes.

_____ 3. A sometimes perceptive, energetic, ferretlike Scotland Yard inspector.

_____ 4. The long-suffering landlady of Baker Street.

_____ 5. A New Jersey-born prima donna. To Holmes, always *the* woman.

_____ 6. London's "Napoleon of crime."

_____ 7. Sherlock Holmes's elder brother.

_____ 8. A street urchin who sometimes spoke for the Baker Street Irregulars.

_____ 9. The "Notting Hill murderer" who escaped from Dartmoor Prison.

_____ 10. The "Solitary Cyclist."

_____ 11. Assumed name of Holmes's informant inside the Moriarty organization.

_____ 12. Watson fell in love with her in *The Sign of the Four* and married her soon after.

_____ 13. Pawnbroker who joined the Red-Headed League.

_____ 14. The "worst man in London."

_____ 15. He witnessed Moriarty's death at Reichenbach Falls and tried to avenge it.

Solutions: 1. Billy; 2. Stamford; 3. Lestrade; 4. Mrs. Hudson; 5. Irene Adler; 6. Moriarty; 7. Mycroft; 8. Wiggins; 9. Selden; 10. Violet Smith; 11. Fred Porlock; 12. Mary Morstan; 13. Jabez Wilson; 14. Milverton; 15. Moran

The Adventure of the Naval Treaty

First Publication:

The Strand Magazine, October and November 1893

Principal Predicament:

Watson's old Cambridge chum, Percy "Tadpole" Phelps, is in trouble. A rising star in the Foreign Office, he'd been given responsibility to copy a top-secret document—a naval treaty between England and Italy. Phelps promised to take precautions to safeguard the papers until they could be handed over the next day. That night, alone in the office, he was midway through copying the document when he began to feel drowsy. He rang the bell to ask the night commissionaire to bring him a cup of coffee. He was surprised when the commissionarie's wife answered the bell and took his order, but thought little of it and continued his work. After a period, he got up and ventured down the hall to find out what was taking so long with the coffee, and found the commissionaire asleep with the kettle boiling furiously. He was about to awaken the man when he heard the service bell. It was ringing from the room where he'd left the secret treaty, half-copied, on his desk. He feared the worst, and, racing back to the room, found his fears justified. The treaty was gone. It's been ten weeks since the treaty was stolen, and Phelps has spent most of that time in bed, growing weaker and paler by the minute. Hearing the story, Holmes walks to an open window where he contemplates a moss rose and falls into a reverie.

Oddities and Discrepancies:

Some very fussy Sherlockians have found fault with Holmes for his poetic rhapsody about flowers because he made the false statement that "its smell and its color are an embellishment of life," when, in fact, the smell and color of flowers have practical functions for the insects that fertilize them.

C A P S U L E

The Adventure of the Final Problem

First Publication:

The Strand Magazine, December 1893

Principal Predicament:

"It is with a heavy heart that I take up my pen to write these the last words in which I shall ever record the singular gifts by which my friend Mr. Sherlock Holmes was distinguished." So writes Watson, and there's no mystery here. We know that, by the end of this story, we will learn of the death of Sherlock Holmes. Before that fateful scene, however, Watson records a genuine cat-and-mouse game, with the Napoleon of crime, Professor Moriarty, in hot pursuit. Holmes thoughtfully assesses the life he's lived, telling Watson, as the two hike through the Alpine countryside, "I have not lived wholly in vain. If my record were closed tonight I could still survey it with equanimity. The air of London is the sweeter for my presence. In over a thousand cases I

"I saw Holmes with his back against a rock and his arms folded, gazing down at the rush of waters." Illustration by Harry Edwards, 1893.

am not aware that I have ever used my powers on the wrong side." These are the musings of a man ready to die if he must, in his attempt to capture or kill the "most dangerous and capable criminal in Europe."

Notable Feature:

When this story was published, readers' reaction was swift and bitter. People of London wore black armbands in a display of public mourning and canceled their subscriptions to *The Strand* by the thousands. Conan Doyle later reported, "If I had killed a real man I could not have received more vindictive letters than those which poured in upon me."

Oddities and Discrepancies:

Contemplating the presumed plunge of Moriarty and Holmes over Reichenbach Falls, Watson states categorically that "any attempt at recovering the bodies was absolutely hopeless." Yet, water flowing over the Falls becomes part of the Aare, which eventually empties into the Lake of Brienz, where a corpse would most likely float to the surface.

CAPSULE

The Hound of the Baskervilles

—⁓—

FIRST PUBLICATION:

The Strand Magazine, from August 1901 to April 1902

PRINCIPAL PREDICAMENT:

Illustration from an Hungarian translation of The Hound of the Baskervilles–A Sátá Kutyája.

Dr. James Mortimer of Grimpen, Dartmoor, brings to Baker Street a document dated 1742 which he reads aloud in a high, cracking voice. It is the legend of the Hound of the Baskervilles. Holmes yawns and dismisses it as a fairy tale, so Dr. Mortimer pulls out of his pocket a more recent document–a clipping from the *Devon County Chronicle,* which reports the sudden death of Sir Charles Baskerville. Holmes is still not interested, not, that is, until Dr. Mortimer tells him that near the body of Sir Charles were found footprints–not of a man, not of a woman, but of a gigantic hound. Encouraged by the glimmer of curiosity he's sparked in the great detective, Dr. Mortimer begs advice about what to do with Sir Henry Baskerville, the heir to the dead man's estate, who will be arriving at Waterloo Station in little over one hour. Isn't there evidence of a diabolical agency that makes Dartmoor an unsafe abode for a Baskerville? Holmes promises to mull over the problem, and mull he does, brooding for some hours in his armchair while consuming large amounts of coffee and smoking vast quantities of tobacco. Just after breakfast the following day, Dr. Mortimer returns to Baker Street, accompanied by Sir Henry, who reports that a joke has been played on him that very morning. He's received a one-sentence letter at his hotel, with words cut and pasted from a newspaper, which reads, "As you value your life or your reason keep away from the moor." Only that, and nothing more.

NOTABLE FEATURE:

Written after Holmes's supposed plunge over Reichenbach Falls, Conan Doyle predated this adventure rather than resurrect the fallen detective. Nevertheless, the reading public went wild for the story, and it remains, easily, the most famous and beloved of all the Sherlock Holmes stories.

The Adventure of the Empty House

First Publication:

Colliers, September 1903

Principal Predicament:

In the spring of 1894, all of London is buzzing with news of the Park Lane Mystery concerning the murder of the Honorable Ronald Adair, an easygoing young aristocrat. Most puzzling is the fact that Adair has been shot and killed in a room locked from the inside. Watson, still missing and mourning Holmes, takes an evening stroll that leads him to the site of the crime. In the crush of the crowd, Watson accidently bumps into a white-whiskered bibliophile, who drops a volume titled *The Origin of Tree Worship.* When the apologetic doctor retrieves the book, the old man snarls and disappears into the throng of curiosity seekers. After Watson returns to his Kensington home, he's astonished when the maid announces a visitor–the old book collector. In the course of a brief discussion of books, Watson glances away for a moment. When he turns back, the old man has revealed himself to be none other than Sherlock Holmes in disguise. At this, Watson faints for the first time in his life, but he soon recovers to the full realization that Holmes is alive and well. He's delighted to hear Holmes announce that a dangerous night's work lies ahead for them. After Holmes explains to Watson what he's been doing during the three years he was presumed dead, the game is, once again and very blessedly, afoot indeed.

Oddities and Discrepancies:

Though astute readers can poke numerous holes in this adventure, no one really cares about the inconsistencies for, after all, Holmes has returned.

A knowledge of Japanese wrestling saved Holmes's life at Reichenbach Falls.

English Crime (and Its Napoleon)

It is a matter of no small curiosity that the exploits of Sherlock Holmes, inextricably tied in the public mind with crime, take place in a society where crime was undergoing a substantial and long-term decline. More curious yet, many stories involve no crime at all; in others Holmes lets criminals escape the law; in some he even (perish the thought) breaks the law himself.

Horace Walpole could bemoan in 1782 London's "enormous profusion of housebreakers, highway-men and footpads. . . . One dare not stir out after dinner but well-armed." But an official known as London's Criminal Registrar in 1901 noted that in recent decades "we have witnessed a great change in manners . . . a decline in the spirit of lawlessness."

It is not that London lacked promi-nent incidents of crime. The "Jack the Ripper" murders started in 1888, the same year *Study in Scarlet* was pub-lished. Other famous criminal cases of the period included Dr. Edward William Pritchard, convicted of poisoning his wife and mother-in-law in Glasgow in 1865, and Dr. Crippen, an American dentist convicted of poisoning his wife in 1910 in London's Camden Town. ("When a doctor does go wrong he is the first of criminals," Holmes remarks in "The Adventure of the Speckled Band.")

Comparable statistics are difficult to come by and even more difficult to rely upon. But many experts agree with the criminologist James Q. Wilson that while the level of crime and disorder in the Western world's large cities and industrializing nations was very high in the early decades of the nineteenth cen-tury, it "decreased substantially during the latter part of that century."

This phenomenon seems to contra-dict many explanations about the cause

Professor Moriarty turned his rounded back on Holmes and went peering and blinking out of the room. Illustration by Sidney Paget

of crime, including a widening economic and social gulf between the classes. For the more immediate causes of the decline, many look to the introduction of widespread street lighting in London, beginning in the early part of the century; the clearing of a number of notorious rookeries or slums in various urban renewal schemes; and the creation of the Metropolitan Police in 1829, replacing the ineffective "watch" system of local pensioners and volunteers.

Moriarty and Moran

Most police and other professionals in the criminal justice system recognize crime as an essentially decentralized and unorganized phenomenon. Yet the mythic power of the concept of *organized* crime has had substantial resonance with both modern and nineteenth century readers.

The late twentieth century witnessed the widespread popularity of the

Godfather saga; its equivalent in some respects can be found in the Sax Rohmer novels of the criminal mastermind Fu Manchu, popular in England and America early in the century; their precursor in many ways was Conan Doyle's infamous Professor James Moriarty, author of *The Dynamics of an Asteroid* and other mathematical arcana.

Despite how large he looms in the mythology of Holmes and in sequels, spin-offs and broadcast versions, Moriarty plays a surprisingly small role in the Canon. He is mentioned in only a handful of stories, prominent in only two. Much of what we know about him comes from the early passages of *The Valley of Fear* in which Holmes is the recipient of information about a pending case from an informer in Moriarty's organization. Moriarty himself has no real role in the story.

Holmes, however, uses the occasion to instruct Scotland Yard on the brilliance of Moriarty's mind, the scope of his operations, the depths of his depravities, and the disingenuity of his harmless appearance.

Described by Holmes as "the Napoleon of crime," Moriarty was "the organizer of half that is evil and of nearly all that is undetected in this great city. He is a genius, a philosopher and abstract thinker. . . . He sits motionless, like a spider in the center of its web, but that web has a thousand radiations and he knows every quiver of each of them."

In "The Adventure of the Empty House," a story that followed Moriarty's apparent death in a titanic struggle with Holmes ("The Final Problem"), he was recalled by Holmes as "a man of good birth and excellent education . . . with a phenomenal mathematical faculty." So compelling was a treatise he wrote on the Binomial Theorem that he won at the age of twenty-one a university chair, but "hereditary tendencies of the most diabolical kind . . . increased and rendered infinitely more dangerous by his extraordinary mental powers" led him from his university town to the criminal underside of London.

"For years I have been conscious of some power behind the malefactor, some deep organizing power which for ever stands in the way of the law. . . . I have felt the presence of this force, and I have deduced its actions in many of those undiscovered crimes in which I have not been personally consulted," said Holmes. "For years I have endeavored to break through the veil which shrouded it, and at last the time came when I seized my thread and followed it, until it led me, after a thousand cunning windings, to ex-Professor Moriarty of mathematical celebrity."

> "I make a point of never having any prejudices, and of following docilely wherever fact may lead me."
> —*The Adventure of the Reigate Squires*

The Second Most Dangerous Man. . . .

The companion of Professor Moriarty's efforts was Colonel Sebastian Moran, his chief of staff. Very much the man of action rather than intellect, Colonel Moran was the son of a British diplomat and had served with distinction in India with the Empire's forces.

However, he was compelled to leave India and the service by pending scandal, ending up in Moriarty's admittedly remunerative employ, being used only for "one or two high-class jobs, which no ordinary criminal could have undertaken."

Like his employer, Moran was an author, admittedly in a somewhat different genre: *Heavy Game of the Himalayas,* and *Three Months in the Jungle;* he was said to have been the best heavy game shot in the Eastern Empire and was regarded by Holmes as "the second most dangerous man in London."

It was Moran—"the brow of a philosopher above and the jaw of sensualist below" in Watson's phrase—who murdered the Honorable Ronald Adair to forestall being revealed as a cheat at cards, and he who made a very nearly successful attempt on Holmes's life in "The Empty House."

While Moriarty is never heard of again, save for an occasional plaintive reference from Holmes about the decline of the class of English criminals in his absence, Moran apparently survived for some years despite his arrest. He is referred to in the present tense by Holmes in "His Last Bow" at the outbreak of World War I in 1914.

The "fourth smartest man in London" had much in common with him. John Clay, who makes his only appearance as the criminal mastermind in "The Red-Headed League" had like Moran, respectable, even noble antecedents. Moran's father was Sir Augustus Moran, C.B.; Clay's grandfather was a Duke; both were educated at Eton and Oxford; both apparently endured long tenures as guests of Her Majesty thanks to Holmes's efforts.

Real-Life Models

In making his case to Scotland Yard Inspector Macdonald for Moriarty's centrality in London's criminal world, Holmes mentions as a model the case of Jonathan Wild, though he misdates Wild's tenure to somewhat later in the eighteenth century than was the truth. "Wild was the hidden force of the London criminals, to whom he sold his brains and his organization on a fifteen percent commission," Holmes tells Macdonald.

Wild, who supposedly learned his trade in debtor's prison, organized thieves and other felons, and operated as a fence for stolen goods. Criminals who resisted his organizing efforts were betrayed to the police, and dozens were said to have gone to the gallows on his leaked information. Unmentioned by Holmes was a similarly renowned organizer and fence, Ikey Solomons, said to have been the model for Fagin in *Oliver Twist,* who operated in Spitalfields in East London in the first half of the nineteenth century. However, there is a mention in "The Adventure of the Mazarin Stone" of an Ikey *Sanders.*

Holmes makes reference also to Charlie Peace in "The Adventure of the Illustrious Client." A famous criminal of the middle decades of the nineteenth century, Peace's renown came more from his intelligence and bravado than his organizing genius. He was an inventor who suggested mechanical improvements to his prison in Dartmoor that were later adopted, and who patented a device for raising sunken vessels. After committing one murder, he wandered England for several years, concealing his identity by using an artificial arm and

hand he had crafted to disguise the fact that he was missing not a hand, but a finger. Described by Holmes (who had some knowledge of the subject) as a violin virtuoso, Peace was eventually apprehended and hanged for murder in 1879.

In Pursuit of Justice

From his comment in "The Adventure of the Cardboard Box" that "I chose to only associate with those crimes which present some difficulty in their solution," we have a significant clue about Holmes's own rationale for his work.

As noted above, a number of Holmes's cases involved either no crime at all or a relatively minor infraction. These include "The Man with the Twisted Lip," "The Adventure of the Yellow Face," "The Adventure of the Noble Bachelor," "A Case of Identity," "The Adventure of Shoscombe Old Place," "The Adventure of the Missing Three-Quarter" "The Adventure of the Creeping Man" and "The Adventure of the Blanched Soldier," among others.

In stories such as "The Boscombe Valley Mystery," "The Adventure of the Priory School," "The Adventure of the Sussex Vampire," and "The Adventure of the Abbey Grange," having identified the miscreant, Holmes makes no attempt to inform the official police of the results of his inquiries.

Adding to these potential misprisions of felonies, in "A Scandal in Bohemia," "The Adventure of the Illustrious Client" and "The Adventure of Charles Augustus Milverton," among others, he bends or completely breaks the law, including burglary and the destruction of evidence.

For it was not the law Holmes represented. "I am not retained by the police to repair their deficiencies," he tells Watson in "The Adventure of the Blue Carbuncle." And like many people of his profession, he had an affinity for the criminal mind, "I have always had the idea that I would make a first-class criminal," he remarks in "Charles Augustus Milverton."

In the last analysis, the puzzle having been solved to his satisfaction, Holmes weighed the impact of public knowledge of the details of the crime where circumstances were extenuating and real justice could be imperiled.

"I think," he told Watson after Milverton's demise, "there are certain crimes which the law cannot touch, and which, therefore, to some extent, justify private revenge."

P U Z Z L E R

If You Can't Say Anything Nice. . . .

London's official crime-fighting force is known generically as Scotland Yard, after the site of the first headquarters of the London Metropolitan Police. "Official" detectives from Scotland Yard or one of the regional police forces play a role in most stories in the Canon–but rarely to Holmes's praise. Match the statement by Holmes to the "copper" he describes.

1. "You have instinct and intuition."

A. Inspector Hopkins (Abbey Grange)

2. "It is a pleasure to work with you."

B. Inspector Lestrade (Cardboard Box)

3. "If you wish to get on in your new duties you will work with me, not against me."

C. Inspector Forrester (Reigate Squires)

4. "Were he but gifted with imagination, he might rise to great heights in his profession."

D. Inspector Gregson (A Study in Scarlet)

5. "He and Lestrade are the pick of a bad lot."

E. Inspector Forbes (Naval Treaty)

6. "_____ has called me in seven times, and each time his summons has been justified."

F. Inspector Gregory (Silver Blaze)

7. "He is not a bad fellow, though an absolute imbecile in his profession."

G. Inspector Peter Jones (Red-Headed League)

8. "Although he is absolutely devoid of reason, he is tenacious as a bulldog."

H. Inspector Baynes (Wisteria Lodge)

Solutions: 1-H; 2-C; 3-E; 4-F; 5-D; 6-A; 7-G; 8-B

PUZZLER

Agents of an Untimely Demise

Match the weapon to the story in which it plays a key role.

blowgun and dart

Empty House

harpoon

Abbey Grange

revolver

Sign of the Four

jellyfish

Speckled Band

sheath knife

Resident Patient

poker

Charles A. Milverton

air gun

Six Napoleons

hangman's noose

Lion's Mane

swamp adder

Silver Blaze

horseshoe

Black Peter

Solutions: blowgun and dart–*Sign of the Four*; harpoon–Black Peter; revolver–Charles A. Milverton; jellyfish–Lion's Mane; sheath knife–Six Napoleons; poker–Abbey Grange; air gun–Empty House; hangman's noose–Resident Patient; swamp adder–Speckled Band; horseshoe–Silver Blaze

The Adventure of the Norwood Builder

First Publication:

Collier's, October 1903

Principal Predicament:

John Hector McFarlane is about to be charged with murdering Jonas Oldacre, an eccentric and financially successful builder. The *Daily Telegraph* has already printed vigorous headlines. According to the news account, a fire alarm was sounded when a stack of dry wood in the timber yard behind Oldacre's house was entirely consumed by fire. Later, it was discovered that, not only was Oldacre missing, but charred remains were found in the ashes. Police also discovered signs of a murderous struggle in Oldacre's bedroom—his safe was open and papers were scattered about, and there was blood on a walking stick belonging to the handsome, flaxen-haired McFarlane. When uniformed policemen arrive at Baker Street to arrest

In Frederic Dorr Steele's illustration, what should have been "the well-marked print of a thumb" became a bloody hand print.

McFarlane and take him into custody, Holmes persuades Inspector Lestrade to let the pale gentleman finish telling his story. That's when Holmes learns that, just the day before he disappeared, Oldacre had prepared his will, leaving everything to young McFarlane, whom he'd never met.

Notable Feature:

The use of a thumbprint as a clue marks the story as very modern, according to Sherlockian researcher Christopher Redmond, who has pointed out that this story was published in 1903 and Scotland Yard only began officially using fingerprinting in 1901.

Quotable Quote:

Holmes: *"London has become a singularly uninteresting city since the death of the late lamented Professor Moriarty."*

The Adventure of the Dancing Men

First Publication:

The Strand Magazine, December 1903

Principal Predicament:

Someone is scribbling lines of little dancing men on the property of Mr. Hilton Cubit, a Norfolk squire and the honest heir of Ridling Thorpe Manor. The hieroglyphics are unnerving his American wife Elsie, who, one month prior, was seen throwing a letter into the fire. "I have had some very disagreeable associations in my life," she had confided the day before her wedding, and added, "I wish to forget all about them." But someone has come along with a piece of chalk and a need to remind her of the past. Why else would she drop in a dead faint at the sight of the dancing men?

Notable Feature:

This is one of the adventures that Sherlock Holmes does not solve in time. "Would that I had some brighter ending to communicate to my readers," writes Watson. Also, in this story we learn that Dr. Watson plays billiards with someone named Thurston.

Quotable Quote:

Holmes: *"It is not really difficult to construct a series of inferences, each dependent upon its predecessor and each simple in itself. If, after doing so, one simply knocks out all the central inferences and presents one's audience with the starting-point and the conclusion, one may produce a startling, though possibly a meretricious, effect."*

Like other men and women of his day, Watson enjoyed playing billiards.

Oddities and Discrepancies:

According to Sherlockian scholar William S. Baring-Gould, Ridling Thorpe is a combination of the names of two English villages, Ridlington and Edgingthorpe, which Conan Doyle knew well, but where is the New York Police *Bureau*? Even in Doyle's day it was called the New York Police *Department*.

CAPSULE

The Adventure of the Solitary Cyclist

First Publication:

Collier's, December 1903

Principal Predicament:

Through a newspaper advertisement, Violet Smith and her mother met Carruthers and Woodley who said they had been friends of Violet's Uncle Ralph. He had died penniless in South Africa, begging his two friends to look after his relatives. Mr. Carruthers suggested Violet become a live-in music teacher for his ten-year-old daughter. On the weekends, Violet went home to her mother. The arrangement worked happily for several months except that, each Saturday and again on Monday, when she pedaled her bicycle to and from the train station along a lonely stretch of road, Violet was sure she was followed by a man with a dark beard. After hearing her story, a worried Holmes broods, "It is part of the settled order of Nature that such a girl should have her followers . . . but for choice

When Violet Smith, a music teacher, realized she was being followed, she was more curious than alarmed. She slowed down her "machine." Illustration by Sidney Paget

not on bicycles in lonely country roads." He sends Watson to investigate, but, before story's end, both Watson and Holmes are brandishing firearms.

Oddities and Discrepancies:

(1) A marriage ceremony in which the bride is not only unwilling, but is physically gagged, would not be recognized by either church or state. Nor would it have been legally binding without a witness. Since he did not care for the legalities, why did Woodley bother to get a marriage license? (2) Why, if the plucky, independent Violet Smith's hands were not bound, did she not simply pull off the gag placed over her mouth? (3) There are two cyclists in this story—Violet Smith and her pursuer. Who, then, is the "solitary" cyclist?

The Adventure of the Priory School

First Publication:

Collier's, January 1904

Principal Predicament:

There are strange goings on at the Priory. The young son of the Duke of Holdernesse and the unpopular Herr Heidegger, the German teacher, are both missing, having climbed out of their respective windows into the moonlit night. Perhaps, it is hoped, the young Lord ran off to see his beloved mother, the Duchess, living estranged from her wealthy husband in the south of France. But when the boy's blue cricket cap is found in the van of the Gypsies who camp on the moor, Watson and Holmes follow the scent like two old hounds and find the bloodied body of Herr Heidegger. Concern grows for the lad's safety. And then there are all those cow tracks in the mud, but no sign of cows anywhere.

Oddities and Discrepancies:

When Holmes discovers bicycle tracks on the sodden moor, he utilizes them to tell which direction the bike was going. "The more deeply sunk impression is, of course, the hind wheel. . . . It was undoubtedly heading away from the school." This claim has distressed more than one reader, as it is generally believed that the tracks would look the same either coming from or going toward the school. Generous readers conclude that Holmes had other indications to make his judgment call, clues unrecorded by a negligent Watson.

Behind *This* Great Man There's a . . . Watson

Horse and carriage. Love and marriage. Salt and pepper. Sherlock Holmes and Dr. Watson. The two are forever paired in the public imagination.

This pairing is not of two equals. As surely as the earth's moon is a lesser light than the sun, so too is Watson destined to be the supporting actor to Holmes's starring role.

Watson knows the score, but hesitates to articulate it beyond saying, "I was nearer him than anyone else . . . and yet I was always conscious of the gap between." He is genuinely in awe of the Bohemian of Baker Street, who is, he claims, "the man whom above all others I revere." Revere is a strong word. Synonyms for it are "adore," "honor," "venerate," "worship."

Holmes recognizes the gap too, but he expresses appreciation for the nature of their unequal relationship, about which he says to Watson in *The Hound of the Baskervilles,* "It may be that you are not yourself luminous, but you are a conductor of light. Some people without possessing genius have a remarkable power of stimulating it."

"I am lost without my Boswell," says Holmes in genuine appreciation of his scribe, though he is also frequently critical of Watson's efforts. Readers, at least, are eternally grateful to Watson, for there would be no record of the adventures without his hard work. "I hear of Sherlock everywhere since you became his chronicler," says Mycroft Holmes.

Watson has the respect of the master detective. High on the list of qualities Holmes admires in Watson is his absolute and unfaltering trustworthiness. "It makes a considerable difference to me," Holmes says to Watson, "having someone with me on whom I can thoroughly rely."

Then too, there is Watson's common sense. "Good, Watson! You always keep us flat-footed on the ground," says Holmes as he dismisses, out of hand, an uninspired suggestion made by the doctor.

"Count me in, Holmes," Watson says

Watson is always on call, ready to travel at the drop of a deerstalker.
Illustration by Sidney Paget, 1893

in "The Adventure of the Mazarin Stone" adding, "I have nothing to do for a day or two." Though he has a career as a doctor, and, more often than not, family responsibilities to which he must tend as a faithful husband, Watson is ever on call to listen, to act, to travel at the drop of a deerstalker, and then, to reconstruct his notes and fashion the pieces into a cohesive whole. And he follows orders–fetching the dog in *The Sign of the Four,* a brandy and soda for a fainting client in "The Adventure of Wisteria Lodge," and the telephone in "The Adventure of the Three Garridebs." In "The Adventure of the Dying Detective," Watson hides behind the head of Holmes's bed when the detective pleads: "Quick, man, if you love me! And don't budge, whatever happens–whatever happens, do you hear? Don't speak! Don't move! Just listen with all your ears."

The Drawbacks for Watson

"My dear Watson," says Holmes, "you are most long-suffering."

Watson waits for Holmes. Holmes does not wait for Watson. Watson enters the Baker Street flat quietly, assesses the situation, determines the great detective's mood before interrupting. "My friend hardly glanced up as I entered," he writes in "The Naval Treaty," "and I, seeing that his investigation must be of importance, seated myself in an armchair and waited." Another time Watson wrote, "I had no glimmer of what was in his mind, nor did he enlighten me, but sat lost in thought."

Watson is at Holmes's disposal, and

glad to be there. "I was a whetstone for his mind," he writes. "I stimulated him. He liked to think aloud in my presence. His remarks could hardly be said to be made to me–many of them would have been as appropriately addressed to his bedstead."

People entering the Baker Street flat address Holmes and routinely raise an eyebrow at Watson's presence or ignore him altogether. Holmes, of course, speaks in defense of Watson's presence, even insists on it saying, "Have no fear . . . Dr. Watson is the very soul of discretion."

Illustration by Sidney Paget, 1893

And, like a child, Watson abides by the "should be seen and not heard" rule of conduct, waiting for his turn to speak. He writes, "After his habit he said nothing, and after mine I asked no questions. Sufficient for me to share the sport and lend my humble help to the capture without distracting that intent brain with needless interruption."

Where Holmes indulges in complexity, Watson is bound to be simple. Genuinely happy with the good things of life—a hard day's work, a friendship, a home, a wholesome woman to love, he demonstrates courage, loyalty and compassion time and again but almost always in the background.

Where Holmes toys sleepily with drugs when bored by the world, Watson warns about addiction and bad habits. He is the voice of reason, the adult to Holmes's child. When bad boy Holmes leaves a messy room, Watson prods him to clean it up. Where Holmes is reckless, Watson is on guard, protective, alert. He's the one who worries. He does not act on whim.

When Holmes affects a been-there, done-that, jaded, world-weary air, Watson brings fresh astonishment to each curious turn of events. Inclined to accept the situation at face value, he's easily fooled, as he is by Holmes a number of times. While he takes it all in stride, his ego is damaged again and again.

"I have no doubt that I am very stupid," he says, "but I must confess that I am unable to follow you." And again he writes:

> I trust that I am not more dense than my neighbors, but I was always oppressed with a sense of my own stupidity in my dealings with Sherlock Holmes. Here I had heard

what he had heard, I had seen what he had seen, and yet from his words it was evident that he saw clearly not only what had happened, but what was about to happen while to me the whole business was still confused and grotesque.

The Chosen One

The benefit, for Watson, is that it is exhilarating to be the one "chosen" by the luminary around whom the action revolves, even if it means being chosen to pick up the crumbs from the luminary's table.

Watson recognizes in Holmes the excitement of the unpredictable, the fantastical, the important. He knows he is privileged to be in on the adventure. Anyone might walk through their Baker Street door—pauper or king. Watson would not, could not, generate the outrageous experiences he has with Holmes. This is high drama. Without Holmes, Watson's life would be far less interesting, if not downright mundane. His life is an adventure as long as he's the one chosen by Holmes.

And Watson *is* the chosen one. It is to him Holmes appears early one frosty morning, as described in "The Adventure of the Abbey Grange," with the immortal words, "Come, Watson, come! . . . The game is afoot. Not a word. Into your clothes and come!"

The Sherlock Holmes
Mystery Map of Southern England

Violet Smith, the Solitary Cyclist, is followed whenever she bikes the six lonely miles from Chiltern Grange to Farnham.

Someone has ransacked Mary Maberley's villa, The Three Gables. Poor Mary. Her morose son died just last month.

Violet Hunter, governess at Copper Beeches, is uneasy aboaut her employers' demand that she cut her hair short. Holmes admits he's more nervous in this smiling countryside then in the villest alleys of London.

At Riding Thorpe Manor on the Norfolk coast, scribbled lines of Dancing Men have appeared on Hilton Cubit's doors and window sills.

In a cottage at Norbury, a strange Yellow Face appears in an upper window.

Moral exemplar Grace Dunbar sits in a cell, accused of murdering a Brazillian beauty at Thor Bridge.

NORFOLK

Prize-winning Silver Blaze has disappeared and the horse's trainer is found dead on the moor.

Farnham **London**

Winchester

Croydon

Dartmoor

SUSSEX

Placid-faced Susan Cushing of Croydon has received a Cardboard Box containing a gruesome surprise—two human ears, freshly severed.

The butler has vanished from the Manor House of Hurlstone. Holmes suspects the answer is in the Musgrave Ritual. Whose is it? His who is gone. Who shall have it? He who will come.

What's that howling on the bleak and lonely Dartmoor? It must be the devlish Hound of the Baskervilles.

In retirement on the Sussex downs, Sherlock Holmes enjoys bee farming.

The Adventure of Black Peter

First Publication:

Collier's, February 1904

Principal Predicament:

As the story begins, Holmes, chuckling over his coffee cup, informs Watson that he's been out early, stabbing a pig carcass with a huge "barbed-headed spear." It was all to solve the mystery of Woodman's Lee. Before he can explain further, Inspector Hopkins arrives at Baker Street. He reports that no progress has been made in the case of Captain Peter Carey, whose body was found pinned to the wall of his cabin by a harpoon. The discovery of a notebook bearing the initials J.H.N. soon has Holmes and his partners in the case hiding in the bushes to ambush the nocturnal visitor at the scene of the bloody crime. John Hopley Neligan came in search of Captain Carey, whom he believed might know why Neligan's father vanished at sea. Now the Captain is dead and Neligan's notebook is covered with blood. He is arrested for the crime, but Holmes knows something the police don't: it's hard to drive a harpoon through dense flesh.

Oddities and Discrepancies:

Why did Holmes spend three days in wiring to Dundee for a crew list of the *Sea Unicorn?* We know from a previous story that there was a telephone across the road. Why didn't Holmes use it to call the Dundee police for the information?

C A P S U L E

The Adventure of Charles Augustus Milverton

First Publication:

Collier's, March 1904

Principal Predicament:

Holmes and Watson take the law into their own hands in their efforts to prevent the repulsive Milverton (Holmes calls him "the worst man in London") from blackmailing the beautiful but desperate Lady Eva Brackwell. She does not have enough money to purchase her freedom from Milverton's harassment, and the scandal about to descend on her will most certainly mean the end of her wedding plans. In the little time he has to find a solution for Lady Eva, Holmes disguises himself as a workman and courts Milverton's housemaid while plying her for information.

The worst man in London.
Illustration by Sidney Paget

Notable Feature:

Holmes and Watson break the law and keep mum about another lawbreaker in order to honor a higher good. When directly asked to assist the police, Holmes boldly tells Lestrade, "My sympathies are with the criminals rather than with the victim, and I will not handle this case."

Oddities and Discrepancies:

(1) How can Holmes be so sensitive to the distress of Lady Eva and be so hard-hearted toward the agony of Agatha, Milverton's housemaid, jilted by the disguised detective? Even Watson is appalled. (2) Watson records that, at the close of their night of crime, he and Holmes, pursued on foot, "dashed away across the huge expanse of Hampstead Heath." By Watson's estimate, they ran two miles before stopping. Some researchers have pointed out, however, that Hampstead Heath is neither two miles long nor two miles wide.

The Adventure of the Six Napoleons

First Publication:

Collier's, April 1904

Principal Predicament:

"You wouldn't think there was anyone living at this time of day who had such a hatred of Napoleon the First that he would break any image of him that he could see," says Lestrade. Holmes, bored by mere madness, sinks back into his chair until the inspector mentions the burglary involved. Someone is breaking into homes and offices throughout London and smashing plaster busts of Napoleon. Lestrade suspects the Mafia. Watson waxes eloquent on the limitless possibilities of "monomania." A melancholy journalist, victim of the plaster smasher, agrees it must be a case of sheer lunacy.

Notable Feature:

For once, Watson is asked what he thinks about a case and indulges in a lengthy bit of speculation from his readings of French psychology.

Quotable Quote:

Holmes: *"The Press, Watson, is a most valuable institution, if you only know how to use it."*

Oddities and Discrepancies:

A photograph, a key item of evidence, is found in a dead man's pocket. Holmes not only has the temerity to want to hold onto it, but Scotland Yard lets him do so.

The Adventure of the Three Students

First Publication:

The Strand Magazine, June 1904

Principal Predicament:

When Mr. Soames left for tea at four-thirty, half a chapter of Thucydides, the text for the next day's Greek translation exam, was on his desk at the College of St. Lukes. When he returned, it was gone. If the stolen text is not found by the next morning, the examination will have to be postponed and a hideous scandal will throw a cloud over the whole university. Whoever stole the exam must also have left those tiny, black, puttylike pyramids scattered about. Three of the students with rooms near the office are under suspicion. And then there's Bannister, the servant whose honesty is above suspicion.

Quotable Quote:

Holmes: *"Not one of your cases, Watson--mental, not physical."*

Oddities and Discrepancies:

Thucydides seems an odd test choice for a passage of Greek translation that the students have not seen. As many critics have pointed out, this examination is for the Fortescue Scholarship, and any candidate for this scholarship would be well versed in Thucydides.

*Illustration by
Frederic Dorr Steele for
Collier's Magazine,
Sept., 1904.
Credit: Airmont
Publishing Co., Inc.*

Parodies, Pastiches, and Other Forms of Flattery

—⊱⊰—

If imitation is the sincerest form of flattery, then Sherlock Holmes has been flattered most sincerely indeed. The world's first consulting detective, whose earliest appearance in print was Christmas 1887, captured the popular imagination so effectively that within five years his name was already a household word.

Playful Parodies

Sherlock Holmes was a name that would be twisted and turned inside out and upside down with impunity, as it was in the 1892 parody "The Adventures of Sherlaw Kombs," penned by Detroit journalist Luke Sharp (pseudonym of Robert Barr).

Scottish novelist James M. Barrie (who, as noted, would later write *Peter Pan*) delighted his dear friend Conan Doyle with an early spoof in which Holmes bluntly tells his creator an unpleasant truth and is promptly turned into a ring of smoke. As the banished Sherlock Holmes drifts slowly to the ceiling, he cries out to Doyle, "Fool, fool! I have kept you in luxury for years. By my help you have ridden extensively in cabs, where no author was ever seen before. Henceforth you will ride in buses!"

Just a month before devoted fans would curse the story line that led to Reichenbach Falls, "The Umbrosa Burglary" appeared in the November 4, 1893, issue of *Punch*. The story, by "Cunnin Toil," alias Rudolf Chambers Lehmann, a Member of Parliament, featured a bevy of agitated females and inquisitive males, and a detecting duo–the sagacious Picklock Holes and his scribe Potson.

In William Kahn's wicked spoof, "The Succored Beauty," Oilock Combs is busy impressing his faithful confidante Dr. Spotson with an extraordinary exhibition of observation, when the two are interrupted by a sharp knock on the door. It is the distressed Duchess of Swabia who cries, "I am lost!" The quick-thinking and fleet-footed Combs bounds down the stairs, then up again and informs his client that she is not lost, but is currently at No. 62 Fakir Street. "My savior!" cries the duchess.

In "The Unmasking of Sherlock Holmes" by Arthur Chapman, the master detective is confronted by his predecessor in the literary world, Dupin, Edgar Allan Poe's creation. Monsieur Dupin points out some uncanny parallels in their circumstances:

> I am out of sorts with fortune and so are you. I am always smoking when thinking out my plans of attack, and so are you. I have an admiring friend to set down everything I say and do, and so have you. I am always dazzling the chief of police with much better theories than he can ever work out, and so are you.

All of this leaves the Baker Street bachelor mopping his brow and looking at Watson "shamefacedly as a schoolboy who has been caught with stolen apples in his possession."

Another unmasking of sorts happens in P. G. Wodehouse's story, "From a Detective's Notebook" in which Holmes is revealed to be . . . well, let's just say some might call him the "Fiend of Baker Street."

The American writer O. Henry (pen name of William Sydney Porter) author of "The Gift of the Magi," lampooned the world's first and only consulting detective in "The Adventures of Shamrock Jolnes," and Bret Harte, best known for his short stories about the American West, mocked the tobacco aficionado in a story about Hemlock Jones of Brook Street whose adoring confidante writes, "I at once threw myself in my usual familiar attitude at his feet."

Even Sir Arthur Conan Doyle joined in the fun. He penned one parody in the early 1920s for inclusion in a doll house designed for Her Majesty. The miniature mansion, 39 inches in height, had working electric lights and running water. Postage-stamp-sized paintings were done by British masters, and, in the library, were tiny books written by the greatest British authors of the day, including Rudyard Kipling, Thomas Hardy, and Joseph Conrad. In Conan Doyle's gently amusing, if diminutive, tale "How Watson Learned the Trick," the good doctor tries desperately to best his breakfast partner, and, inevitably, fails.

The parodies and spoofs have continued through the years, with a variety of authors having fun with variations on the famous name. In *A Spaniard in the Works,* published in London in 1965, the late John Lennon seems to have wandered through a Lewis Carroll looking glass in whimsical word play about Shamrock Womlbs who, in the "ear of our Loaf 1892" exclaims, "Ellifitzgerrald my dear Whopper" while out in the dark streets prowls the relentless Jack the Nipple.

In "The Adventure of the Dog in the Knight" (the title itself a spoof to delight Sherlockians), Robert L. Fish gives the world *Schlock Homes* of 221-B Bagel Street and his sidekick Watney. They ponder the fate of Sir Gibbon, who died after eating a frankfurter.

Another clever tale is Martin H. Ornstein's witty "The Adventure of the Soiled Sanctuary," set in 1534. Here, Brother Whitsun of the Holy Order of Poor Bakers shares his cell with Brother Alms. Nicknamed "Shire Luck," Alms

"Rat!" he cried in penitence, "you're a wonder!" Illustration from The Wind in the Willows.

has a penchant for unraveling mysteries from the most minute clues. As the story opens, his help is sought in Italy where a holy well once attracted many pilgrims before it was desecrated and the water was turned foul. By story's end, Shire Luck Alms and Brother Whitsun have listened sympathetically to an artist's tale of what Alms calls "a three-pope problem" and have concluded that "it was Michelangelo Buonarroti who tainted the sealing of the Cistern Chapel."

Beyond Human Form

Holmes has been parodied in a vari-ety of animal guises. In one chapter of the beloved children's classic *The Wind in the Willows* by Kenneth Grahame, Mole plays Watson to Rat's Holmes in "The Singular Adventure of the Unexpected Doorscraper." In this adventure, Rat and Mole are lost in a markerless snow-covered wilderness until Mole trips on something which Rat properly deduces to be the entrance to Mr. Badger's home.

The Mole fell backwards on the snow from sheer surprise and delight. "Rat!" he cried in penitence, "you're a wonder! A real wonder, that's what you are. I see it all now! You argued it out, step by step, in that wise head of yours, from the very moment that I fell and cut my shin, and you looked at the cut, and at once your majestic mind said to itself, 'Door-scraper!' . . . You're simply wasted here, among us fellows. If I only had your head, Ratty. . . ."

In Poul Anderson's science fiction story "The Martian Crown Jewels," Holmes's descendent, "Syaloch," is a storklike, seven-foot biped with a long-beaked face and a triplanetary clientele. He maintains a thorough collection of criminological literature including Martian books, Terrestrial micros, and Venusian talking stones. When asked how he feels about Earthlings, the tobacco-loving Martian replies, "I have no prejudices. It is the brain that counts, not whether it is covered by feathers or hair or bony plates."

In "The Curious Computer," written by English author Peter Lovesey and included in *The New Adventures of Sherlock Holmes,* Grievous awakens his bed-mate Silicon Lil at 4 A.M. to watch a top-secret video smuggled out of the New Scotland Yard. It's about a computer program—the Home Office Large Major Enquiry System—HOLMES. According to the video, HOLMES is "the most valuable aid to the detection of crime since fingerprints were classified. . . . No member of the criminal fraternity can sleep easily now that Holmes is working for the Yard." Grievous and Lil can't get back to sleep.

> **"Jealousy is a strange transformer of characters."—*The Adventure of the Noble Bachelor***

The Canon Continued–the Art of the Pastiche

If parody is fun, pastiche is more popular, and literally thousands of stories have been written beyond the original Canon of official Sherlock Holmes stories. The series stories with recurring characters and settings, a form perfected by Doyle, lends itself to the ongoing creation of tales that could have been found in Watson's tin dispatch box. Edgar W. Smith explained, "There is no Sherlockian worthy of his salt who has not, at least once in his life, taken Dr. Watson's pen in hand and given himself to the production of a veritable adventure."

Serious students rank these continuations of the Canon into strict categories, for which the highest regard is given to those labeled "orthodox pastiche." This term, as explained in a scholarly treatise "Reloading the Canon" by Larry Feldman, refers to "the extent to which the writer is attempting to duplicate Doyle so precisely as to make his story stylistically indistinguishable from those in the Canon."

Noteworthy is "The Man Who Was Wanted," a pastiche so convincing that, when it appeared in print in the late 1940s, it was believed to be a previously unpublished "lost" work by Conan Doyle himself—the sixty-first story of the Canon. It had been found among Doyle's papers and the confusion was understandable. It was eventually revealed that the story was by Arthur Whitaker, who had sold it to Sir Arthur for ten guineas for possible use as a story idea.

"The Adventure of the Unique Hamlet" by Canadian-American essayist Vincent Starrett, is an "orthodox pastiche" regarded by some as the finest ever written. In it, book collector Harrington Edwards collapses in 221-B Baker Street as he tells the doctor and the detective about how he was mugged the night before. He was on his way home after borrowing a priceless book–the original manuscript of Shakespeare's *Hamlet*. The mugger took off with the rare volume, and now the book collector is quite beside himself.

Another Shakespearean character makes an appearance in the two-act play, *Sherlock Holmes and the Hands of Othello* by Alexander Simmons. The play revolves around Ira Aldridge (1805–67) the first African-American (later British) Shakespearean tragedian. Holmes confronts the ghost of Othello, dressed in the robes of a Moorish general.

August Derleth (1909-71), an American author, deserves special note. He has been called "the greatest serious imitator of the master" and "the king of the pastiche writers." Derleth created a series of tales parallel to the Canon, which feature a Holmes-like consulting detective, Solar Pons of Praed Street, and his secretary-sidekick, Dr. Parker. These stories, set between World War I and II, are highly regarded because they are close in tone to the original canonical stories.

Holmes and History

Holmes and Watson encounter actual figures from history, most often Jack the Ripper, the one great unsolved real-life mystery from Victorian London in a number of pastiches, including Ellery Queen's *A Study in Terror,* Edwin Hanna's *The Whitechapel Horrors,* and *The Last Sherlock Holmes Story* by Michael Dibdin.

If, in the popular imagination, Jack the Ripper is evil unrevealed, Hitler is evil's personification. One pastiche inspired by the Nazi horror is "The Return of Francois le Villard" by Tony Seton. In this story, Holmes and Watson travel to Berlin in 1934 in a time machine created by H. G. Wells to stop Hitler. "Never," says Holmes, "have I felt such danger."

In *The Case of the Revolutionist's Daughter: Sherlock Holmes Meets Karl*

THE CASE OF THE
REVOLUTIONIST'S
DAUGHTER

SHERLOCK HOLMES
MEETS KARL MARX

by
Lewis S. Feuer

*Illustration by Gregory Lyde Vigrass
Prometheus Books, reprinted by permission
of the publisher.*

Marx by Lewis S. Feuer, Holmes is set the task of finding Marx's daughter Eleanor, a leader of the women's socialist international and active trade union organizer, who has mysteriously disappeared. Holmes delves into the world of such real-life socialist intellectuals as George Bernard Shaw and Beatrice [sic] Potter, grappling with their various revolutionary arguments, propositions, hopes and dreams in his search for the missing Eleanor. Holmes is never won over to the socialist point of view, but at book's end, after solving this mystery, Holmes "was consulted quite frequently by revolutionists in all sorts of predicaments. They knew he had no sympathy with either their political aims or their methods, but they valued highly what they oddly called his 'dialectics.' Holmes could never manage to get them to explain to him what was meant by that word."

In *Sherlock Holmes and the Titanic Tragedy* by William Seil, Holmes and Watson accompany a government courier who is transporting secret plans for a new submarine across the Atlantic. As readers anticipate disaster, Holmes's adventure takes him into every nook and cranny of the legendary ship and he meets a number of its famous passengers.

In *The Boer Conspiracy* by John C. Woods, Holmes and Watson scramble to prevent the assassination of Winston Churchill, and in *The Seventh Bullet* by Daniel D. Victor, the duo find themselves in New York City rubbing elbows with Theodore Roosevelt and William Randolph Hearst on a mission to deter the assassination of an American journalist.

Michael Hardwick's acclaimed pastiche, *The Prisoner of the Devil,* pub-lished in 1980, has Holmes coming to the defense of Alfred Dreyfus, a French artillery officer unjustly accused of selling military secrets to Germany.

Sarah Bernhardt and Sherlock Holmes are both visiting Rio de Janeiro in one Brazilian pastiche, *O Xangô de Baker Street* by Jô Soares, a story in which Holmes searches for a stolen Stradivarius.

Sherlock Holmes and the Mysterious Friend of Oscar Wilde by Russell Brown opens with the arrival of "the High Priest of the Decadents" at 221-B Baker Street where he refuses Mrs. Hudson's command to wait below, because "the hallway wallpaper is so ghastly." Wilde is wearing pale lavender gloves that match his spats and he's holding a lily. Holmes proclaims, "My interest in flowers is limited to opium, poisons, and belladonna–in all of which useful properties the lily is deplorably deficient," to which Wilde retorts, "Pity, I think it is better to take pleasure in a flower than to pursue indiscreet revelations of its life underground." With this exchange, the tone is set for the two Victorian gentlemen to contrast their points of view even as they are drawn together to clear the name of Holmes's page-boy, Billy.

Perhaps the most famous pastiche featuring an historical figure is *The Seven-Per-Cent Solution* by novelist/screen-writer Nicholas Meyer, in which Sigmund Freud is called upon to unlock the mystery of Holmes's past. In a sequel, titled *The Canary Trainer,* Holmes has gotten off Freud's couch and traveled to Paris. Here, his virtuosity on the violin lands him a job as a pit musician at the Paris Opera, and he again encounters the enchanting con-

Holmes and Watson pursue Edward Hyde, who has disappeared from the pages of Robert Louis Stevenson's story. Written by Gordon Rennie, illustrated by Woodrow Phoenix. Credit: Woodrow Phoenix/Tundra Publishing

tralto who bested him in *A Scandal in Bohemia,* Irene Adler, to Holmes always *"the* woman."

As in the book just described, a number of pastiche writers involve Holmes with other fictional characters. In *The Holmes-Dracula File* by Fred Saberhagen, the Victorian sleuth does battle with Count Dracula, as he does in Loren Estelman's *Sherlock Holmes vs. Dracula or the Adventure of the Sanguinary Count.*

In an unusually sophisticated and exquisitely rendered comic book,

Sherlock Holmes in The Curious Case of the Vanishing Villain, by author Gordon Rennie and artist Woodrow Phoenix, a distressed Dr. Henry Jekyll appears at Baker Street with an appeal for help. Edward Hyde has disappeared from the pages of his own story. Conan Doyle's doctor and detective take the case and race through strangely empty London streets only to find that Hyde has escaped Robert Louis Stevenson's "tedious tale" across the threshold of nightmares and into the more exciting hallucinogenic landscape of Edgar Allan Poe.

Completing the Canon

Filling in the gaps in the Canon is the favorite task of many who pen pastiches. What was the truth about Holmes's childhood and early education? What was he really doing while Watson was investigating the mysterious hound of the Baskervilles? What actually happened to Holmes during the Great Hiatus when Watson and the world thought he was dead?

The Sherlockian scholar William S. Baring-Gould created an account of Holmes's life from womb to tomb in *Sherlock Holmes of Baker Street: A Life of the World's First Consulting Detective.* Michael Harrison, a scholar of British history and student of the Canon, penned a convincing biography complete with actual photographs of the detective in *The World of Sherlock Holmes.*

The absence of a romance in Holmes's life is unbelievable to some and has led to serious speculation. *Sherlock in Love* by Sena Jeter Naslund, reveals the detective's one great love and the reason this love had to remain unrequited. (It's a good reason.)

The editors of *Holmes for the Holidays* attempt to supplement the only recorded Christmas season adventure in the Canon with stories featuring Holmes and Watson "solving the darkest of crimes in the brightest of seasons."

The escapades enjoyed by Holmes in retirement have proved fertile soil for a number of writers, including Laurie R. King, the award-winning author of several pastiches. In *The Beekeeper's Apprentice,* a Nancy Drew wannabe named Mary Russell finds the retired detective on the Sussex Downs, and the two soon become engaged in a series of adventures. Holmes and Russell are paired again in *A Monstrous Regiment of Women,* concerning an odd feminist church and in *A Letter of Mary,* another pastiche teaming Mary Russell and her mentor, who pore over first-century papyrus from the town of Magdala in the Holy Land.

Watson and Holmes are not the only ones who live on in the popular imagination. Other characters from the four novels and fifty-six short stories that make up the Canon take center stage in a number of pastiches. Mrs. Hudson, landlady of the stately tread, writes to Dr. Watson from her address at 221-A Baker Street to describe strange goings-on in her tenant's rooms in Ardath Mayhar's "The Affair of the Midnight Midget." She reminisces about the old days at Baker Street in "Mrs. Hudson Speaks" created by actress ZaSu Pitts.

In *Enter the Lion* by Michael P. Hodel and Sean M. Wright, Holmes's older brother Mycroft has an adventure and gives the reader a glimpse of the young Sherlock before he teamed up with Watson.

"Dr. Watson, Mr. Sherlock Holmes" The Adventures of Young Stamford and Other Sherlockiana, by Richard M. Caplan, M.D., is the biography of the character who was destined to introduce the detecting duo (in a chemical laboratory in London's St. Bartholomew's Hospital) and then disappear on page three.

The irresistible Irene Adler, who so fascinated Holmes, is fascinating as well to the writers of pastiche. The only woman to outwit Sherlock Holmes is featured in several books by Carole Nelson Douglas, winner of the American Mystery Award for Best Romantic Suspense Novel.

What was in Watson's tin dispatch box locked in the vaults of Cox & Co. in Charing Cross? And what of Holmes's investigations mentioned but unrecorded by the overworked Watson, such as the "bogus laundry affair," the "repulsive story of the red leech," the "theft of the black pearl of the Borgias," and the story of the giant rat of Sumatra "for which the world is not yet prepared"?

This is fertile soil for many authors, not the least of which was Doyle's youngest son who, it is said, sat at his father's desk to expand the Baker Street saga. In *The Exploits of Sherlock Holmes* by Adrian Conan Doyle and John Dickson Carr, the adventures cursorily mentioned in Watson's chronicles are here recorded, each with the references to the cases as they appeared in the Canon.

The unrecorded adventures are also the impetus for the highly regarded stories by June Thomson in *The Secret Files of Sherlock Holmes* and *The Secret Chronicles of Sherlock Holmes*. An unchronicled story is tackled in Richard L. Boyer's bluntly titled, *The Giant Rat of Sumatra*. The rat's tale is also treated in an unusual collection edited by Marvin Kaye, *The Resurrected Holmes,* in which modern American mystery writers pull off a "double pastiche" by penning purportedly canonical Sherlock Holmes adventures in the idiosyncratic

> **"It is a capital mistake to theorize before one has data. Insensibly one begins to twist facts to suit theories, instead of theories to suit facts."**
>
> **—*A Scandal in Bohemia***

manner of such noted writers as H. G. Wells, P. G. Wodehouse, Theodore Dreiser, and Jack Kerouac.

In the mid-1940s, radio broadcasts of stories based on the unchronicled cases of Sherlock Holmes kept listeners enthralled. Week after week they tuned in to hear the voices of Basil Rathbone and Nigel Bruce in original radio dramas written by Denis Green and Anthony Boucher. Over forty years later, Ken Greenwald—who remembered as a kid snuggling under the bed covers after lights out and listening to the radio adventures of Sherlock Holmes and Dr. Watson—rewrote the plays in short story format and presented them under the title, *The Lost Adventures of Sherlock Holmes.*

The Fictional Sir Arthur

Holmes and his entourage are not the only ones featured in these further adventures. Sir Arthur Conan Doyle himself has been a character in works of fiction. In the supernatural adventure thriller, *The List of 7* by *Twin Peaks* cocreator Mark Frost, an ensemble of villains attempt to open a door from the other world so that Satan may reign upon the throne of England for a thousand years. Doyle is the central character in the story that records events in his early career.

William Shatner, the actor who portrayed Captain Kirk in the *Star Trek* series, is listed as the author of *Believe,* a novel about the troubled friendship of Conan Doyle and Harry Houdini.

Conan Doyle is also teamed with Houdini in *Escapade* by Walter Satterthwait as the two try to solve a locked-room murder mystery.

Sir Arthur, who did, in fact, believe in and write about fairies late in his life, appears briefly as a manipulative, dishonest character in Steve Szilagyi's offbeat novel, *Photographing Fairies.*

In *The Piltdown Confession* by Irwin Schwartz, a devious, underhanded Conan Doyle is involved in a historic hoax. In 1908 in Sussex, England, the fossilized remains of what were believed to be the "missing link" between humans and apes was unearthed and studied by anthropologists and paleontologists until it was proved in 1953 that the jaw belonged to an orangutan.

The Baker Street Beat Goes On

Neither parody nor pastiche, a number of books involve characters who are devoted fans and artistically inspired by Sherlock Holmes. Such books include Julian Symons's mystery, *A Three Pipe Problem* about an actor who has built his fame on the dramatization of Sherlock Holmes, and *The Barker Street Regulars: A Dog Lover's Mystery* by Susan Conant. In this novel, Holly Winter takes her trained malamute Rowdy on a visit to Gateway Nursing Home where she meets ninety-year-old Althea Battlefield, a passionate Sherlockian.

Canonically Inspired Kid Lit

Delving into mysteries and secrets has long been a staple of children's literature, and for this reason, Sir Arthur Conan Doyle's creations have inspired a

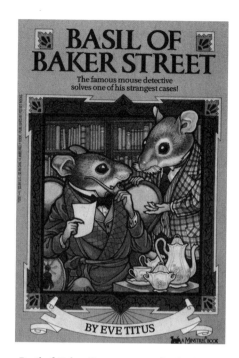

Basil of Baker Street, *written by Eve Titus, cover illustration by Judith Sutton Credit: Judith Sutton*

number of imitators. In *Sherlock Chick's First Case,* the main character is hatched from his egg, complete with a detective's hat and magnifying glass. After nothing more than a mere ruffle of his new feathers, Sherlock Chick sets out to find who has stolen the corn from the chickens' feed bin.

Eve Titus created a whole series about "Basil of Baker Street." In her books, Basil, "the Sherlock Holmes of the Mouse World," lodges with Dr. David Q. Dawson below the famed *human* detective, in the cellar community of Holmestead. Basil learns detective lore by listening at his hero's feet and taking notes in *shortpaw.* Dr. Dawson, also a mouse, has reason to believe that the human Holmes is charmed by his wee imitator in the deerstalker cap. When the first *Basil* mystery was published, Adrian Conan Doyle wrote to Ms. Titus, "May I offer you my heart-felt congratulations. It is a simply wonderful creation, and I can assure you that my father would have reveled in every page."

In "A Study in Garlic" by Eric and Stephen Dalton with illustrations by Susan Dalton, published in *Holmes for the Holidays,* a periodical "for the young mystery fan," Purrlock Holmes and Watnip are glad they are not up against Professor Meowiarty, "a mastermind of feline evil, the ultimate criminal genius of all catkind." Of course, Inspector Hisstrade from Scratchland Yard wants credit for solving the case, as usual.

In the *Nate the Great* series by Marjorie Weinman Sharmat, a young detective dons trench coat and deerstalker, speaks in Sam Spade sentences, and indulges his love of pancakes as he and his dog Sludge traipse through the neighborhood solving kid-sized mysteries. "I have found lost balloons, books, slippers, chickens," Nate brags. "Even a lost goldfish."

For older children there is *The Disappearance of Sister Perfect* by Jill Pinkwater. In this novel, Sherelee Holmes, who claims to be the great, great granddaughter of the famed detective, sets out to save her obnoxious sister Myra from the Temple of Perfection. Along the way, she is aided by her best friend, Joan H. Watson. "Every great detective should have an admiring friend and biographer," says Sherelee, "who is able to record exploits, feats of mental brilliance and acts of bravery. It sounds like bragging when the detective is forced to write about herself." Unfortunately, English is Joan Watson's worst subject, she can't spell or punctuate, but she is trustworthy. "Great detectives learn to adapt to circumstances beyond our control," shrugs Sherelee.

Holmes for the Holidays *is a periodical published by The Chester Baskerville Society, 1415 Swanwick Street, Chester, IL 62233. Illustration by Bob Weber, Jr.*

Canines of the Canon

———✦✦✦———

A menagerie of animals, large and small, exotic and mundane, grace the pages of the Sherlock Holmes stories. There's a baboon, a badger, and an infamous snake. There's a cheetah, a cat, and a cormorant. There's a giant rat and there's Silver Blaze, a horse of course. Dogs, however, hold a special place in the Canon–those that howl and those that remain silent.

Top dog is the heinous hound that haunts the Baskerville family, that demon of the moor about whom legends abound. As the story is outlined in the faded document brought to 221-B Baker Street and read aloud in a high, crackling voice by Dr. Mortimer, the ghostly beast first appeared in the 1700s to avenge a damsel in distress. According to the story, Hugo Baskerville, a wild, godless, cruel man, abducted the daughter of a local yeoman one night when the woman's father and brothers were away. Lust-driven, he held her captive in an upper chamber of Baskerville Hall while he drank with his wicked companions, anticipating the cat-and-mouse game yet to come. The shivering woman anticipated the game as well, and decided to attempt a daring escape. In terror, she climbed down the ivy that covered the south wall and headed out over the moor.

When Hugo discovered that his cage was empty, he went into a rage and set his hounds on the woman. Then he mounted his black mare and took off in pursuit. His drunken companions followed, but when they saw Hugo's black mare galloping across the moor without its rider, they knew something was very wrong. Soon after, they came to a horrific scene–the maid dead of fear and fatigue, the hounds whimpering and slinking away, and Hugo Baskerville, belly up, with a great blazing-eyed, black hound standing over him and tearing at his throat. Hearing the story, Holmes is not impressed, until Dr. Mortimer tells him the news–the hound is back.

Holmes seems to know and respect the faithful behavior of various mutts and, on a number of occasions, observes them for clues to the strange goings-on of his human subjects. Most notable of these observations is the one Holmes makes in "Silver Blaze," about the curious incident of the dog in the nighttime. When it's pointed out that the dog in question did nothing in the nighttime, Holmes remarks, "That was the curious incident."

In "The Adventure of the Creeping Man," Holmes is thinking of writing a small monograph "upon the uses of dogs in the work of the detective." As he considers the facts of the case at hand he muses, "A dog reflects the family life. Whoever saw a frisky dog in a gloomy family, or a sad dog in a happy one? Snarling people have snarling dogs, dangerous people have dangerous ones. And their passing moods may reflect the passing moods of others." And so the question presents itself, "Why does Professor Presbury's wolfhound, Roy, endeavor to bite him?" The dog, once affectionate and devoted to his human companion, has now been banished to the stables, where he languishes in chains. By the end of the story, after Holmes and Watson hide in the bushes and observe the dog by moonlight, Holmes credits the dog for being aware of the situation earlier than all the humans involved.

Holmes takes his cue, again, from the unusual behavior of a dog in "The Adventure of Shoscombe Old Place" –this time a beloved black spaniel. In this case, the little dog gives a joyous cry and dashes toward the carriage in which its mistress is supposedly riding. When the dog's eagerness turns to rage and snapping jaws, Holmes explains to Watson, "He thought it was his mistress and he found it was a stranger," and proclaims, "Dogs don't make mistakes."

The detective is put on the right path another time by witnessing the sad fate of Carlo, the unfortunate spaniel in "The Adventure of the Sussex Vampire." When the dog is observed walking toward his master with its tail on the ground, Holmes is told that the vet has diagnosed the paralysis as spinal meningitis. This bit of information about the dog confirms what Holmes has already suspected about the case.

In "The Adventure of the Lion's Mane," Holmes's old housekeeper interrupts the retired detective's musings with the news that Mr. McPherson's dog has died "of grief for its master." It seems the dog stopped eating the day its master was found dead after a swim in the Channel and now the dog, too, has been found dead at the very place. The detective's ears perk up! He ponders, "That the dog should die was after the beautiful, faithful nature of dogs. But 'in the very place'! Why should this lonely beach be fatal to it?" He hurries to view the dead dog where he finds "the faithful little creature, an Airedale terrier, laid out upon the mat in the hall. The body was stiff and rigid, the eyes projecting, and the limbs contorted. There was agony in every line of it." It's a sad fate for the devoted canine, but provides a valuable clue for Holmes.

At the beginning of his career, described in "The Adventure of the 'Gloria Scott,'" while still at university, Holmes was bitten by a dog, a bull terrier. He was subsequently "laid by the heels for ten days" during which time the dog's master, Victor Trevor, routinely stopped by to check Holmes's progress. Thus formed the one and only real friendship Holmes can remember from his college days.

Illustration by Paget.

Though the doctor/detective duo is responsible for the deaths of several dogs in the course of their many adventures, at times, canines are trusted and skilled associates, accomplices in the crime-solving business. In *The Sign of the Four*, Holmes employs Toby, a queer mongrel with a most amazing power of scent about whom he says, "I would rather have Toby's help than that of the whole detective force of London." He's loaned to Holmes in order to track the murderers of Bartholomew Sholto.

According to Watson, Toby is "an

THE ADVENTURE
of the
MISSING THREE-QUARTER

Holmes with Pompey—"the pride of the local draghounds." Illustration by Frederic Dorr Steele

ugly, long-haired, lop-eared creature, half spaniel and half lurcher, brown and white in color, with a very clumsy, waddling gait." With the encouragement of a little sugar, Toby accompanies Watson back to the scene of the crime and to Holmes who pushes a creosote handkerchief under the dog's nose with the command, "Smell it, Toby, smell it!" Toby considers the fabric "with a most comical cock to its head, like a connois-seur sniffing the bouquet of a famous vintage," and then he's off, hot on the trail at a pace that keeps Holmes and Watson at the top of their speed. When suddenly the dog becomes the "very picture of canine indecision," waddling in circles and looking up at the detective "as if to ask for sympathy in his embarrassment," Holmes is the one to growl, "What the deuce is the matter with the dog?" But Holmes is good-humored and sufficiently amused by the dog and even indulges in a fit of laughter with Watson before continuing the pursuit of the felons.

Toby is not the only helpful pup. In "The Adventure of the Missing Three-Quarter" we meet Pompey, "a squat, lop-eared, white-and-tan dog, something between a beagle and a foxhound." Holmes tells Watson that the dog is "the pride of the local draghounds–no very great flier, as his build will show, but a staunch hound on a scent." He then addresses the dog, "Well, Pompey, you may not be fast, but I expect you will be too fast for a couple of middle-aged London gentlemen, so I will take the liberty of fastening this leather leash to your collar. Now, boy, come along, and show what you can do."

In *A Study in Scarlet*, Watson watches Sherlock Holmes investigate the scene of the crime with his tape measure and a large round magnifying glass.

> As I watched him, I was irresistibly reminded of a pure-blooded, well-trained foxhound, as it dashes backward and forward through the covert, whining in its eagerness, until it comes across the lost scent.

In the same story, Holmes himself even says, "I am one of the hounds and not the wolf."

Outside the Canon, Holmes has been portrayed by dog-characters several times, notably by Carl Schultz's

Holmes tested a poison pill on a dying terrier in A Study in Scarlet. *Illustration by George Hutchinson, 1891.*

Snoopy from the *Peanuts* comic strip and on television by the PBS after-school-series dog *Wishbone.*

Finally, there is the mystery of Watson's claim, in *A Study in Scarlet,* that he keeps a bull pup. The bulldog is never again mentioned in the stories, nor does it make an appearance. This fact may give credence to the claim made by Sherlockian researcher Jack Tracy that the phrase, "to keep a bull pup," was, in Victorian times, an Anglo-Indian saying that meant to have fits of quick temper. Mystery solved.

The Adventure of the Golden Pince-Nez

First Publication:

The Strand Magazine, July 1904

Principal Predicament:

When the maid found poor Willoughby Smith breathing his last on the study floor, he was clutching a golden pince-nez and muttering, "The professor–it was *she.*" Professor Coram has already decided that the maid must have heard wrong. "Susan is a country girl, and you know the incredible stupidity of that class." He concludes that his secretary committed suicide. But as Holmes joins the professor in smoking cigarette after cigarette and observes the professor's increased appetite, he tells Hopkins to be on the lookout for a woman with a thick nose and rounded shoulders.

Illustration by Frederic Dorr Steele, 1904

Quotable Quote:

Holmes: *"What did you do, Hopkins, after you had made certain that you had made certain of nothing?"*

The Adventure of the Missing Three-Quarter

First Publication:

The Strand Magazine, August 1904

Principal Predicament:

The big game with Oxford is the next day, and fortunes are riding on the outcome. Cambridge doesn't stand a chance without its star three-quarter, Godfrey Staunton. Staunton, however, is nowhere to be found. Cyril Overton, skipper of the rugby team, had already made the rounds to make sure his men were in bed when the porter at Bentley's hotel saw Staunton run off with a rough-looking bearded stranger. He hasn't been seen since. Just hours before his disappearance, Staunton dispatched a telegram to someone with the message, "Stand by us for God's sake!" As the case unfolds, Holmes and Watson find themselves stranded and friendless in an inhospitable town, but, before long, Holmes is on the trail of the missing athlete, with the help of Pompey, a lop-eared, white and tan hound.

Notable Feature:

At the beginning of this tale, Watson ponders Holmes's drug mania, recognizing that the craving is not dead but sleeping, easily awakened in times of calm. By the end of the tale, however, he has reason to be glad that Holmes still carries a syringe.

The night he disappeared, Godfrey Staunton appeared pale and bothered and complained of just a touch of headache.

The Adventure of the Abbey Grange

First Publication:

The Strand Magazine, September 1904

Principal Predicament:

Lady Brackenstall has a story to tell. The night before, three intruders had assaulted her in her home, knocked her unconscious, used the bell rope to tie her to a chair and gagged her with a handkerchief. When her husband responded to the commotion, he was brutally struck down. The police have already decided that the fiends are the infamous Randall gang, a father and two sons who have been wreaking havoc in the area. But Holmes is not so sure. His brain clicks off the inconsistencies in the lady's story and he soon tells her that he believes her account to be an absolute fabrication. He's right, of course.

Quotable Quote:

Holmes: *"Come, Watson, come! . . . The game is afoot. Not a word. Into your clothes and come!"*

"These glasses do puzzle me, I confess."
Illustration by Frederic Dorr Steele, 1904

The Adventure of the Second Stain

First Publication:

The Strand Magazine, December 1904

Principal Predicament:

The Premier of Britain and the Secretary for European Affairs have a top-secret assignment for Holmes: find the long, thin, pale blue envelope sealed in red wax with the stamp of a crouching lion. It has been stolen from a locked box kept on the Secretary's bedside table. The statesmen assure Holmes that recovery of the letter is crucial for the well-being of all Europe. This is not enough for Holmes, however, who politely declines the assignment, unless the statesmen are willing to tell him the exact nature of the letter. Backed into a Baker Street corner, they agree with the terms and confide to Holmes and Watson that the let-ter, written by a certain foreign potentate whose feel-ings had been ruffled, is so provocative that, if pub-lished, it would lead to a great war and the expenditure of a thousand millions and the lives of a hundred thou-

According to Watson's narrative, Lady Hilda Trelawney Hope was the most lovely woman in London.

sand men. Holmes suspects the mysterious Eduardo Lucas might know some-thing about the stolen letter, but learns from the newspaper that Lucas has been murdered the night before. Holmes lingers at the crime scene as the pieces fall into place. On the verge of solving the mystery, two things are clear–the Secretary's overprotected, gorgeous wife is taking her husband's crisis very hard, and someone repositioned the rug the dead Lucas lay on. But why?

Notable Feature:

Holmes, who has retired and taken up bee farming, only consents to let Watson publish this story when it is argued that it was the most important inter-national case that he was ever called upon to handle, and it should at last be laid before the public.

Oddities and Discrepancies:

Would the statesmen have trusted such a sensitive letter to a bedside box if its discovery held the potential for utter catastrophe for millions of people?

Colonial Adventures: "You Have Been in Afghanistan. . . ."

⟨≈⟩

To contemporary American audiences the British Empire is little more than a background for *Masterpiece Theatre* productions; even for most contemporary English readers the Empire is a historical reality rather than a presence in their everyday lives.

But to people in Conan Doyle's day, in Great Britain, America, or almost anywhere else in the world, the British Empire was a profound geopolitical and economic fact of life.

The colonies were a source of both raw materials and a market for manufactured goods; as such they helped make England the preeminent economic power on the planet. That economic strength, along with the army and particularly the navy that had helped establish and defend those colonies, made the relatively small nation of Great Britain an equal player with the great powers on the continent, and a decisive factor in the power struggles of many other nations around the world.

The colonies themselves served English society in a number of ways. They provided thousands of young English men (and some women) with a chance to break out of England's still highly stratified social and economic structure; their unsettled nature and less law-abiding environments offered an outlet for the "dangerous" classes (Australia started out as a penal colony after all); and in what had become the relatively orderly and predictable Victorian England, they offered the new, the exotic, and the decidedly unEnglish.

Wild Colonial Boys

Nearly half the tales in the Canon have some reference to the present and former colonies. Conan Doyle had few equals as a popular storyteller, particularly of stories that might be described as "ripping yarns." The exotic locales and uninhibited societies of the present and former colonies were particularly appropriate for such stories, and it is no accident that they play a large role in three of the four Holmes novels–*A Study in Scarlet, The Sign of the Four,* and *The Valley of Fear.* (The fourth novel, *The Hound of the Baskervilles,* is

Mormon emigrants in the desert.

Native officers of the Bombay Army.

set in the Devon moors, a location as remote, desolate, and exotic as one could find in England.)

The great trends and events of Victorian colonial history are evident in stories such as "The Adventure of the 'Gloria Scott,'" a tale of prisoners revolting aboard a convict ship en route to Australia; *The Sign of the Four* and "The Adventure of the Crooked Man," which include the Indian Mutiny, a midcentury revolt of native troops in British India and an event of enormous popular concern in England; and "The Adventure of the Blanched Soldier" whose critical event takes place during the Boer War in South Africa.

Even Watson's wound, which we learn of in *A Study in Scarlet,* was the result of British army action in colonial conflict in Afghanistan.

India was also the locale where notable villains perfected their villainy. Dr. Grimesby Roylott, the fierce protagonist of "The Adventure of the Speckled Band," had killed an Indian servant in a fit of rage, while Colonel Sebastian Moran, before becoming chief of staff to Professor Moriarty, had been a serving officer and "without any open scandal... had made India too hot to hold him."

The Former Colonies

In a letter to an English friend during an 1894 visit to the United States, Conan Doyle described the American people as "not only the most prosperous, but the most even-tempered, tolerant and hopeful that I have ever known."

He added, "When I see all these folk, with their British names and British tongue, and when I consider

An Afghan warrior.

how far they have been allowed to drift from us, I feel as if we ought to hang a statesman from every lamp post in Pall Mall. We've got to go into partnership with them or be overshadowed by them."

But in his fiction America is the battleground between forces of good and the more or less organized forces of evil, such as the Mormons of Utah in *A Study in Scarlet,* or the Scowrers in the isolated coal towns of Pennsylvania in *The Valley of Fear* (who obviously owe much to the labor movement known as the Molly Maguires).

The same is true for short stories such as "The Five Orange Pips," where the American Ku Klux Klan murders three English gentlemen; "The Adventure of the Dancing Men," where a member of an American criminal gang is responsible for the death of the respectable country squire, Hilton Cubitt; and even "The Adventure of the Red Circle," where Italian anarchists transplanted to New York follow one of their own to London.

Cradling and panning at an Australian gold mine.

The Southern Hemisphere

Australia in the Canon is a place one makes one's fortune, through fair means or foul. It is there that James Armitage of the *Gloria Scott* prospers, and where the Ballarat gang hijacks a gold shipment that would resonate decades later in "The Boscombe Valley Mystery." It is to Australia that the disgraced son of the Duke of Holdernesse goes to seek the fortune he cannot inherit.

But much the same could be said of South Africa, where Sir Charles Baskerville "made large sums of money . . . realized his gains, and returned to England with them." It was the fortune alone that returned to England in "The Adventure of the Solitary Cyclist," since Ralph Smith, its owner, died leaving it all to his English niece, Miss Violet Smith.

Colonial Atmosphere

But with all their possibility for crime and conflict, the colonies also produced much that was worthwhile. The elegant and honorable Lady Brackenstall of "The Adventure of the Abbey Grange" was from Australia; the quiet but gentlemanly Henry Baskerville had been raised in Canada; and the high-spirited but inherently noble Hatty Doran ("a strong nature, wild and free, unfettered by any sort of traditions" according to her husband, the eponymous Noble Bachelor) was born and raised in an American mining camp.

The colonies could also mean a fresh start for those who needed a new reputation rather than a fortune. Philip Green of "The Disappearance of Lady Frances Carfax" found both. "I was a wild youngster," the only somewhat more sedate Green recalls of his days before his sojourn in South Africa, and it is to the Rhodesian police that young Gilchrist in "The Adventure of the Three Students" has decided to go after being disgraced.

"For once you have fallen low," Holmes tells him. "Let us see, in the future, how high you can rise."

The Adventure of Wisteria Lodge

First Publication:

Collier's, August 1908

Principal Predicament:

Holmes himself says of this adventure, "A chaotic case, my dear Watson. . . . It will not be possible for you to present it in that compact form which is dear to your heart. It covers two continents, concerns two groups of mysterious persons." It all begins when the solemnly respectable, gray-whiskered Scott Eccles arrives at Baker Street to report that he has had a most singular and unpleasant experience. Before he can tell his tale, two Inspectors are ushered in by Mrs. Hudson to report that a Mr. Aloysius Garcia, of Wisteria Lodge, has been found dead, with a letter from Eccles in his pocket. When he realizes he is a suspect in a murder, the pompous Mr. Eccles requires a brandy and soda. What eventually unfolds is a story involving dictators and revolutionaries, a broken-hearted woman drugged with opium, a dead white bird, and a bucket of blood. Dr. Watson does his best to weave all this into a cohesive whole and, when he's done, there are no loose threads.

Notable Feature

Collier's published this long and confusing tale in its August 15, 1908, issue, but *The Strand Magazine* chose to publish it in two parts, "The Singular Experience of Mr. John Scott Eccles," and "The Tiger of San Pedro."

Quotable Quote:

Holmes: *"Life is commonplace; the papers are sterile; audacity and romance seem to have passed forever from the criminal world."*

Illustration by Arthur Twidle for the Strand Magazine, *September 1908.*

The Adventure of the Bruce-Partington Plans

First Publication:

The Strand Magazine, December 1908

Principal Predicament:

Published during a period of growing tension in European affairs, this story brings Holmes, at the determined urgings of his brother Mycroft, into the mystery of the death of a young Woolwich Arsenal clerk, Arthur Cadogan West, and the disappearance of the plans for the revolutionary Bruce-Partington submarine. "You must drop everything, Sherlock," Mycroft tells him. "I have never seen the Prime Minister so upset." After some Holmesian undertakings that are at best extralegal if not absolutely criminal, the solution involves foreign spies and the ruin of a fine English family.

Notable Feature:

In this story we are enlightened as to the actual role of Mycroft Holmes in Whitehall. Holmes tells Watson, "You are right in thinking that he is under the British government. You would also be right in a sense if you said that occasionally he *is* the British government."

"The tall and portly form of Mycroft Holmes was ushered into the room. Heavily built and massive, there was a suggestion of uncouth physical inertia in the figure . . ."
Illustration by Sidney Paget

Oddities and Discrepancies:

How is it that Cadogan West's murderer, at a time when the English gallows were "in full swing," drew only fifteen years in prison for his crime?

The Adventure of the Devil's Foot

First Publication:

The Strand Magazine, December 1910

Principal Predicament:

An ailing Sherlock Holmes and his concerned companion are vacationing on the moors at the far end of the Cornish peninsula when two visitors arrive at their cottage with a story of horror. It seems that, the night before, Mortimer Tregennis had enjoyed an evening of playing cards with his sister and two brothers. He had left them seated happily around the table. This morning, however, the siblings had been found, in a strange tableau, still seated at the table, but radically changed. The sister was dead and the two brothers demented, driven mad with terror. Yet, nothing in the room had been altered, nor was there a sign of theft. In the afternoon, Holmes and Watson are visited by the famous lion hunter, Dr. Sterndale, who, given word of the horror, has delayed his trip back to Africa in order to help solve the sinister mystery. The next morning, as Watson is shaving, the vicar returns to the vacationers' cottage in a frantic state crying, "We are devil-ridden, Mr. Holmes! My poor parish is devil-ridden! . . . Satan himself is loose in it!" It seems Mortimer has died of the same symptoms as his poor sister.

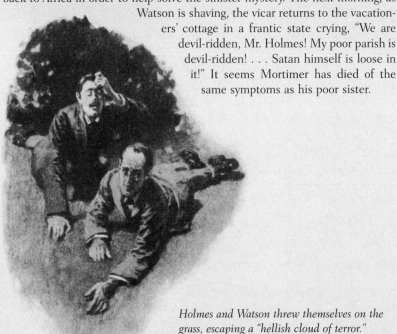

Holmes and Watson threw themselves on the grass, escaping a "hellish cloud of terror."
Illustration by Gilbert Holiday, December 1910.

The Adventure of the Red Circle

First Publication:

The Strand Magazine, March and April, 1911

Principal Predicament:

Illustration by H. M. Brock for the Strand Magazine, *March 1911.*

It takes a bit of flattery but Mrs. Warren, a landlady with "the cunning of her sex," coaxes Holmes into listening to her concern about a new lodger who has not come out of his room for ten days and has spent that time pacing up and down. As per their mutual agreement, his meals are left on a chair outside his door, and when he needs something he prints the word on a slip of paper—SOAP, MATCH. Holmes is intrigued. By a process of reasoning, he soon turns to the agony column in the daily paper where he discovers secret messages he believes may be intended for the mysterious tenant. Before he and Watson can act, however, the landlady is back at Baker Street, upset that someone has been "knocking my old man about." It seems, when Mr. Warren left for work that morning, two men threw a coat over his head and bundled him into a cab. Then they drove him around for an hour before roughly tossing him out on Hampstead Heath. Hearing this, Holmes decides he must get a look at Mrs. Warren's lodger.

Quotable Quote:

Holmes: *"Education never ends, Watson. It is a series of lessons with the greatest for the last."*

Oddities and Discrepancies:

Holmes and Watson observe a secret code sent by a flashing candle and assume the English alphabet is being used. Both sender and receiver, however, speak Italian and would likely use the Italian alphabet, which has no letter K. Would this not affect the coded message?

Orders of Precedence–the Noble and the Common of Nineteenth Century Britain

⟆⟆⟆

Few areas in nineteenth century British life are as confusing to modern non-English readers as that of social class, particularly the nobility, and the role this institution played in Holmes's England.

What, for instance, would be the relationship between the Duke of Holdernesse in "The Adventure of the Priory School" and the Baronet, Sir Charles Baskerville, of *The Hound of the Baskervilles*? And of both to Lord Robert St. Simon, principal character of "The Adventure of the Noble Bachelor," or Grand Duke Wilhelm Gottsreich Sigismond von Ormstein, Grand Duke of Cassel-Felstein, and object of "A Scandal in Bohemia"?

To Holmes they were all one. "The status of my client is a matter of less moment to me than the interest of his case," he told Watson, noting that his correspondence included letters from a fishmonger, a tide-waiter (a minor customs official) and a nobleman "and the humbler are usually the more interesting."

The English nobility, also known as the peerage, consists of the holders of five degrees: Duke, Marquis, Earl, Viscount, and Baron. Four of the five take their names from European, rather than Anglo-Saxon roots. The majority of the ranks were created more than five centuries ago, although the actual titles (Viscount X, Baron Y) are often much less ancient. And many, if not most, of the people described as noble or addressed as Lord are in fact commoners.

In addition, while members of the peerage are generally well off and many are rich, there is no mandatory connection between wealth and title, and the impoverishment (a relative term) of a noble family is far from a rare occurrence.

The Higher Degrees

Duke is the highest rank, falling just below that of prince. The rank was created in England in 1337 by King Edward III and has been closely associated with the royal family ever since.

Charles, the current Prince of Wales, is also the Duke of Cornwall. After King Edward VIII renounced his throne to marry Mrs. Simpson, he and his wife were known as the Duke and Duchess of Windsor, the family name of the current dynasty.

The word *duke* is derived from the Latin *dux,* a provincial military commander. In Europe the rank retains implications of sovereignty–the traditional leader of the city-state of Venice was styled the Doge; Mussolini called himself Il Duce; and in "A Scandal in Bohemia" von Ormstein is not just Grand Duke, but the ruler of the duchy of Cassel-Felstein.

Marquis was in Europe a title given to those who oversaw frontier territories (the marches). It was introduced in England in 1385 to rank below that of duke. The marquis most familiar to American readers is probably the Marquis of Queensbury, sponsor of the Victorian rules governing prizefighting that bear his name.

Earl is the only British title that predates the Norman conquest of 1066. It referred at times to both an under-king in the area ruled by the Danes, or to any man of rank, as opposed to a ceorl or churl, an ordinary freeman. After the Norman invasion earls were assumed to be the equivalent of the European count (originally the latin *comes*), who had the lordship of counties.

It is for this reason that the wives and widows of earls are known as countesses, rather than earlesses. Their younger children–such as Ronald Adair, victim of Colonel Sebastian Moran in "The Adventure of the Empty House"–use the title the Honorable

(Adair was the second son of the Earl of Maynooth).

Viscount (rather than vice earl) and Baron, created in the fifteenth and fourteenth centuries respectively, round out the peerage ranks. The title Baron may be Celtic in origin, and did not necessarily refer to a nobleman, but came to mean so, perhaps because of its implications that its bearers were king's men.

Titled but Not Noble

Baronet and knight are titles of respect and honor, but their holders are not noble and may not, on the basis of these distinctions, sit in the House of Lords. If they have a vocation to politics, they must be elected to the House of Commons (until loyal service or a Cabinet scandal leads to their retirement and elevation to the peerage). The titles are often seen, except perhaps by their holders, as provincial, upper–middle class, and even middle-class distinctions.

The title of Baronet was created by James I early in the seventeenth century and more or less openly sold. Knighthood originated in the designation of those who, in return of a grant of land from the king, owed him military service. Its military component remained officially in force until 1660, though rarely invoked in later centuries.

The provinciality of the baronetcy (along with its hereditary aspect) is illustrated by the case of Sir Henry Baskerville, a bachelor whose death beside "the footprint of a gigantic hound" necessitated a search for heirs. The heir was found to be Charles Baskerville, a Canadian farmer who had not set foot in England since his childhood, but who became a baronet on his uncle's demise.

"He wore a ruddy-tinted suit and had the weather-beaten appearance of one who had spent most of his time in the open air, and yet there was something in his ready eye and the quiet assurance of his bearing which indicated the gentleman," Watson noted.

-A.T.SMITH-

Ascending the Ladder

In earlier times, a man's quickest route to ennoblement was military service, but this has generally been replaced by political service, and most modern peerages are the reward for years of effort on party matters. Titles are granted by the Monarch on recommendation of the Prime Minister.

While it is unlikely that the Prime Minister would recommend or the Queen honor a hundred Anarcho-Syndicalists, in fact there is no statutory limit to the number of peers or limitations on their political philosophies. It was this power of appointment, in fact, that was used to insure the passage of a number of wide-ranging political reforms in the nineteenth and twentieth centuries. The Prime Minister and the Sovereign let it be known that if the House of Lords refused to approve the measures, enough new Lords would be appointed of the appropriate political bent to overwhelm the objectors.

Peerages are usually handed down to the eldest surviving son, but many new Lords are now created as "life peers," meaning that their titles will not survive them.

Titles of the Titled

In formal address a Duke is addressed as Your Grace and a marquis as My Lord Marquis. "I thank your Grace," Holmes tells the Duke of Holdernesse in "The Adventure of the Priory School," although given the Continental differences, he tells the Grand Duke, "Your majesty has indeed committed an indiscretion" in "A Scandal in Bohemia."

Earls, viscounts, and barons must make do with "My Lord." Theoretically, only the actual holders of the titles are noble–their spouses and children, however ancient the lineage or distinguished their service, are commoners unless they have independent claims. In practice, however, spouses and children of nobles are known as Lord or Lady.

In addition, peers often have subsidiary titles. If so, their heirs are known by that designation. Thus the missing schoolboy son of the Duke of Holdernesse is formally referred to as Lord Saltire.

This informal formality can be seen in "The Adventure of the Noble Bachelor." Robert St. Simon, the son of the Duke of Balmoral, consults Holmes

in the case of a wife gone missing on her wedding day. Holmes addresses him as Lord St. Simon, although by some standards he was being far too informal. Not only was the gentleman lacking the title Lord except by courtesy. Strictly speaking, the first son and heir would be Lord St. Simon. As the second son of the Duke, Holmes's client would be Lord Robert St. Simon.

A woman who married a peer took on the title, whatever her antecedents. Thus could a shopgirl become a countess, or a country parson's daughter a duchess, though thanks to dynastic considerations and financial concerns these were more often true in fiction than life. But if a male commoner married the widow of a nobleman, he remained plain Mister, while his wife retained her deceased husband's title.

Getting by on a Few Thousand a Year

There is no direct connection between wealth and an English title, but peers often inherit fortunes with their titles, and in recent centuries, when raising men of modest means to the peerage, monarchs have often granted them property sufficient to support an appropriate lifestyle.

But hard times were and are not unknown to the nobility. The above-mentioned Lord Robert was discommoded by more than the embarrassment of his bride's flight.

"She brought, I understand, a considerable dowry," Holmes said.

"A fair dowry. Not more than is usual in my family."

Yet we know from other sources in

the story that even that "usual" amount would have come in very handy for the St. Simons. It was, the story tells us, "an open secret that the Duke of Balmoral has been compelled to sell his pictures," and that the Noble Bachelor of the story "has no property of his own, save the small estate at Birchmoor."

In "The Naval Treaty," Holmes and Watson have gone to the office of Lord Holdhurst, a member of the Cabinet, as part of their effort to find the missing diplomatic document. "He is a fine fellow," Holmes says of the statesman, "but he has a struggle to keep up his position. He is far from rich, and has many calls. You noticed, of course, that his boots had been resoled."

What Does It All Mean?

If a peerage carried no hereditary estates, it had little value outside its vote in the House of Lords. And a title included with its social status a set of social expectations that were all but impossible to meet unless one was well off.

Yet people continued to seek them. Conan Doyle himself said that while he did not approve of titles, he could understand a man taking one at retirement as a testament to the achievement of a body of work. But he described as "unthinkable" that a "young man should saddle himself with a knighthood, a discredited title." (Sherlock Holmes echoed his reluctance. In "The Adventure of the Three Garridebs" Watson makes a passing reference to Holmes having refused the offer of one.)

By this time knighthood had been conferred on many people of modest significance to English society, including men whose commercial background led them to be described as "in trade."

Conan Doyle was offered a knighthood based not on the Holmes stories or his very popular historical fiction, but in royal gratitude for his work on behalf of British interests during the Boer War in South Africa at the turn of the century, including a book he wrote defending British conduct.

He held firm in his refusal to accept "the badge of the provincial mayor" until his mother reminded him that the King might be offended if he refused.

On August 9, 1902, he became Sir Arthur Conan Doyle.

The Disappearance of Lady Frances Carfax

First Publication:

The Strand Magazine, December 1911

Principal Predicament:

Lady Frances Carfax, a middle-aged beauty of precise habits, has disappeared from Lausanne, a city in the west of Switzerland. Holmes sends Watson, who has been feeling old and rheumatic, to research the situation and report back. Philip Green, a huge, swarthy man with a villainous scowl, has been relentlessly pursuing Lady Frances. When confronted with accusations, he leaps on Watson like a tiger. Then there are the Reverend Dr. Shlessinger and his wife who are missionaries from South America. Watson learns that they have left for London accompanied by Lady Frances. All Holmes wants to know is the shape of the Reverend's left ear. The two detectives are soon reunited at Baker Street once again, on the trail of pawnbrokers and oversized caskets.

Quotable Quote:

Holmes: *"One of the most dangerous classes in the world is the drifting and friendless woman. She is the most harmless and often the most useful of mortals, but she is the inevitable inciter of crime in others. . . . She is a stray chicken in a world of foxes."*

The Adventure of the Dying Detective

First Publication:

Collier's, November 1913

Principal Predicament:

As the story opens, Mrs. Hudson, here described as the long-suffering land-lady to the very worst tenant in London, arrives at Watson's rooms with the news that Sherlock Holmes is dying. When he sees the evidence for himself, Watson agrees that the situation is dire. It seems Holmes has contracted a hor-ribly contagious ailment from the Chinese sailors in the East End. Watson endures Holmes's insults and mad rantings about a world overrun by oysters before being allowed to fetch Culverton Smith, a specialist in this rare disease. All seems dark and hopeless until, at last, the gas is turned up and the room illuminated.

Quotable Quote:

Holmes: *"Malingering is a subject upon which I have sometimes thought of writing a monograph."*

Left: Holmes sent word to Culverton Smith that he'd contracted a disease from the sailors at the docks in London's East End. Credit: National Museum of Labour History

Right: "It was that gaunt, wasted face staring at me from the bed which sent a chill to my heart." Illustration by Frederic Dorr Steele, 1913.

The Valley of Fear

First Publication:

The Strand Magazine, September 1914-May 1915

Principal Predicament:

One of the four Holmes novels, *The Valley of Fear* opens in Holmes's study, and includes in its first pages the longest and most detailed discussion of Professor Moriarty in the Canon. The occasion is a note Holmes has received from an informer in Moriarty's organization, notifying him of the danger to the resident of a house known as Birlstone; even as they translate the informer's cipher Inspector Macdonald of Scotland Yard arrives to inform them that a Mr. Douglas of Birlstone Manor has been found "most horribly murdered." But Holmes's visit to the Sussex home of Mr. Douglas only deepens the mystery of his death. The solution seems to lie in the "singular and terrible narrative" set in America twenty years before, in a coal-mining valley aflame with conflict between the mine owners and the workers.

Notable Feature:

Given its length, *The Valley of Fear* was published serially. It obviously owes a great deal to *The Molly Maguires and the Detectives,* an 1887 volume written by the American detective Allan Pinkerton about labor violence in the Pennsylvania coalfields.

Quotable Quote:

Holmes: *"There should be no combination of events for which the wit of man cannot conceive an explanation."*

His Last Bow

First Publication:

The Strand Magazine, September 1917

Principal Predicament:

It is August 1914, on the eve of World War I. The German agent Von Bork, having insinuated himself among the naive English as a harmless sportsman and bon vivant, has sat at the center of a spider's web of agents, collecting information on their country and its military, and passing it on to Germany. Tonight is the capstone of his career, as he waits the arrival of the difficult but productive spy Altamont, an Irish revolutionary and fanatic hater of things English. Altamont's wire promised "sparking plugs" for Von Bork's car, a code for the naval signals that England's enemies are desperate to obtain. It is an aging Holmes (and Watson) who must intervene.

Notable Features:

(1) This is one of the few stories told not in Watson's voice but in the third person. (2) Holmes's vote of confidence in England–"a cleaner, better, stronger land will lie in the sunshine when the storm has cleared"–was published at a time when the English had suffered terrible casualties in a war where an allied victory was anything but assured. (3) Altamont, *nom de guerre* of the Irish revolutionary agent, was the middle name of Conan Doyle's Irish father, Charles.

Quotable Quote:

Holmes: *"Good old Watson! You are the one fixed point in a changing age."*

From Sovereigns to Shillings, Pounds to Pence

———❦———

When Mary Morstan, in *The Sign of the Four*, stands to inherit half a million sterling, just how much is that? And what is the value of the shilling Holmes gives as a day's pay to each of the ragged street urchins of the Baker Street Irregulars in the same adventure? What did Dr. Watson's half-pay retirement from the army buy him?

Comparisons of the later Victorian personal economy and that of today can be misleading. They had neither Porsches nor VCRs, and their rough historic equivalents, carriages and opera tickets, are not really comparable in terms of cost or value. Still, we can discover some rough equivalents and parallels to our own day.

The pound was the standard unit of currency, worth at the time approximately $5 in U.S. funds. (As recently as the 1960s, Irish cops in New York referred to a $5 bill as "a pound.")

Each pound contained 20 shillings, and each shilling 12 pence, making 240 pence to each pound. There were also other coins, from the farthing, worth 1/4 pence, to the guinea, a gold coin worth at that time just over a pound.

The pound itself was in the form of a note. Its coin equivalent was the sovereign.

What It Bought

While the Baker Street Irregulars must be content with a shilling (25 cents U.S.) each for a day's pay, he offers Constable Rance ten times that much, or a half-sovereign ($2.50) tip for his cooperation in retelling the story of the discovery of the Camberwell murder. Given the relatively modest pay of the English bobby at that time, a half-sovereign would have represented a not insignificant sum.

In "A Case of Identity" we may presume Miss Mary Sutherland's station in life from the fact that she met her missing swain at the Gasfitters' Ball. A small legacy provides her with a hundred pounds ($500) a year, and Holmes remarks that "a single lady can get on very nicely on an income of 60 pounds ($300) a year."

"I could do with much less than that, Mr. Holmes," replies the extremely respectable Miss Sutherland.

In "The Man with the Twisted Lip," the former newspaperman Neville St. Clair described his profession as "arduous work at two pounds ($10) a week." The repellent Hugh Boone, however, earned "twenty-six shillings and fourpence" or about $5.25 for a seven-hour stint of begging, giving him more in two days of mendicancy than St. Clair earned in a week of journalism.

Mrs. Warren's Profession

As for the middle class, in "The Adventure of the Red Circle," the landlady Mrs. Warren asks Holmes's help in solving the mystery posed by her lodger, to whom she had offered two rooms and meals for 2-1/2 pounds ($12.50) per week. The man offered her twice that, or five pounds ($25) per week, if he could have the room "on my own terms."

"I'm a poor woman," she tells Holmes, "and the money meant much to me."

We may presume that Mrs. Hudson, the landlady of 221 Baker Street, fell into roughly Mrs. Warren's economic stratum. Students of the period estimate that rooms similar to those occupied by Holmes and Watson would have cost some three to four pounds a week ($15-$20) with meals for the two of them. Watson, as a physician invalided out of the army, was living on a pension of 11 shillings and sixpence a day (about $3, or just over $20 per week). An even division of expenses with Holmes would have left him about half his income for clothing, entertainment, and incidentals.

For purposes of comparison, Arthur Conan Doyle, in his first year or practice as a doctor in a suburb of the Channel city of Plymouth in 1882, earned an average of three pounds a week or 150 pounds a ($750) a year. He paid about one pound a week, or 50 pounds ($250) for the rent of the house that he used as both home and office.

Comfort and More

To find someone in more comfortable circumstances, we can look to Mycroft Holmes. He draws, we are told, 450 pounds a year and is "indispensable" to the government at Whitehall. Since he goes nowhere but his office, his club, and his modest rooms, we may presume that he has a hard time spending even that much. Mr. Grant Munro, in "The Adventure of the Yellow Face," is a hop merchant. He makes seven or eight hundred pounds a year ($4,000) and his wife has an income of her own.

He and his family live in the suburb of Norbury, in "a nice eighty-pound-a-year villa" ($400) and describes himself as "comfortably well off."

Yet the Canon also includes a number of instances where the characters' circumstances went well beyond mere comfort.

The mysterious foreigner who visits Baker Street at the beginning of "A Scandal in Bohemia" arrives in a coach pulled by a pair of matched horses. "A nice little brougham and a pair of beauties," Holmes observes, looking out the window into the street. "A hundred and fifty guineas ($650-$700) apiece. There's money in this case, Watson, if nothing else."

The will of Sir Henry Baskerville in *The Hound of the Baskervilles* included a number of small bequests and a remaining sum of 740,000 pounds ($3.7 million).

"I had no idea so gigantic a sum was involved," said Holmes.

The half a million pounds ($2.5 million) estimated as the worth of the Agra treasure in *The Sign of the Four* would have made Miss Mary Morstan "the richest heiress in England." But it was not because that was the largest potential legacy.

Even if Miss Morstan had been related to the Baskervilles, it is highly doubtful she could have ended up with their fortune. Under the laws of the period, real property was passed on undivided, and only first-born sons or their survivors could inherit it. Miss Morstan's legacy was so valuable because it was in jewels, not in land, and as a woman it could revert to her. Of course, if she married, it would then in

all probability belong legally to her husband.

Money as Evidence

The liberal use of money is itself a clue that things may not be what they seem. In "The Adventure of Copper Beeches" the governess Miss Violet Hunter is used to a salary of four pounds ($20) a month. "Rank sweating," cries her potential new employer, and insists that she can accept no less than twice that sum, or 100 pounds ($500) a year. She thought it "too good to be true," and like most such things, it was.

In "The Adventure of Silver Blaze" Holmes remarks upon the discovery that a man of moderate means has spent much of a year's salary on a lady friend.

"Liberal as you are with your servants, one hardly expects that they can buy twenty-guinea ($100-$120) walking dresses for their women."

In *The Valley of Fear,* Holmes attempts to demonstrate the evil genius of Professor Moriarty, on the surface a mild-mannered academic living on 700 pounds ($3,500) a year. Holmes points out that in addition to a very expensive painting hanging in Moriarty's study, there is the matter of the astronomical 6,000 pounds ($30,000) a year he pays his chief of staff, Colonel Sebastian Moran (and more, says Holmes, than England's Prime Minister earns).

"That's paying for brains, you see–the American business principal," Holmes adds.

Holmes's personal financial circumstances have been the subject of much speculation. He had obvious advantages of education and upbringing, but he felt it necessary early in his career to look for someone to share his living expenses. Over the years, the stories tell us, grateful clients rewarded him for his work, including the gold snuffbox he received for his efforts in the matter of Irene Adler (though he tells the American millionaire Neil Gibson in "The Problem of Thor Bridge" that "my professional charges are upon a fixed scale").

Yet having found the missing heir of the fabulously wealthy Duke of Holdernesse in "The Adventure of the Priory School," he tells the Duke "I am a poor man."

His 12,000-pound fee in that case, even if divided with Watson, could have helped remedy that condition. Six thousand pounds ($30,000) invested at an unremarkable 3 percent would have yielded 180 pounds ($900) a year, presumably more than enough to have kept him comfortable in retirement with his bees upon the Sussex downs.

PUZZLER

Canonical Number Play

Fill in the blanks with the correct numbers.

A. _____ Orange Pips.

B. Jabez Wilson was paid £_____ a week to copy the *Encyclopaedia Britannica*. (Red-Headed League)

C. Number of steps that led up from the hall to the Baker Street suite._____ (Scandal in Bohemia)

D. _____ Napoleons.

E. _____ Students.

F. Charles Augustus Milverton blackmailed Lady Eva Blackwell for £._____ (Charles Augustus Milverton)

G. _____ Garridebs.

H. Street number of Holmes's and Watson's lodging. _____ (Study in Scarlet)

I. _____ Gables.

J. In "Silver Blaze," Holmes estimated the rate of speed of the train to Exeter as being _____ miles an hour.

K. Sign of the _____.

L. _____nd Stain.

M. Missing _____-Quarter.

N. Directions in the "Musgrave Ritual"–"North by _____ and by _____, east by _____ and by _____, south by _____ and by_____, west by_____ and by _____, and so under." (Musgrave Ritual)

O. Date of the manuscript bearing the legend of the Hound of the Baskerville.

Solutions: A. 5; B. 4; C. 17; D. 6; E. 3; F. 7,000; G. 3; H. 221; I. 3; J. 53-1/2; K. 4; L. 2; M. 3; N. 10, 5, 5, 2, 1, 1; O. 1742

183

The Adventure of the Mazarin Stone

First Publication:

The Strand Magazine, October 1921

Principal Predicament:

Billy, the young but tactful page who has eased Holmes's loneliness, informs Watson that the great detective is hard on a case. He's been using a variety of disguises of late, one day venturing forth as a workman, another as an old woman. It all has to do with the hundred-thousand-pound burglary of the Crown diamond, the great yellow Mazarin stone. Mr. Holmes has even been visited by the Prime Minister and the Home Secretary, the page reports. Though the missing Crown diamond has not yet been found, Billy is confident that his master knows whatever is important to know about the case. He's right, of course, and, happily, by story's end, Holmes has a chance to indulge his "impish habit of practical joking."

Notable Feature:

Who wrote this story? It is one of two canonical tales not narrated by either Watson or Holmes. In fact, it is an adaptation of a play written by Conan Doyle, *The Crown Diamond,* first produced in May 1921.

Quotable Quote:

Holmes: *"I am a brain, Watson. The rest of me is a mere appendix."*

The Problem of Thor Bridge

First Publication:

The Strand Magazine, February and March 1922

Principal Predicament:

The Gold King, Neil Gibson, confesses to Watson and Holmes that he had fallen out of love with his passionate Brazilian wife, Maria, and fallen in love with his children's governess, Grace Dunbar. Realizing the situation, the jealous wife had become crazy with hatred for the younger governess, "and the heat of the Amazon was always in her blood." It is Maria, however, who is found shot to death near Thor Bridge, clutching a note signed by the governess: "I will be at Thor Bridge at nine o'clock." Now the governess sits in a jail cell, all evidence pointing solidly to her. The only problem is, she has such an innate nobility of character, it is inconceivable that she could have done the deed.

*"I can't see the best woman God ever made go to her death without doing all that is possible to save her."
Illustration by A. Gilbert, 1922.*

Notable Feature:

We learn of Watson's tin dispatch box, locked in the vaults of the bank of Cox and Co. at Charing Cross, in which he keeps his notes on Holmes's cases, many of which remain unrecorded in the Canon.

Quotable Quote:

Holmes: *"Some of you rich men have to be taught that all the world cannot be bribed into condoning your offenses."*

The Adventure of the Creeping Man

First Publication:

The Strand Magazine, March 1923

Principal Predicament:

Holmes's query begins, "Why does Professor Presbury's wolfhound, Roy, endeavor to bite him?" Other observers are less interested in the dog's bizarre change of behavior than in the elderly professor's, who fell in love with young Alice Morphy, went away for a fortnight and returned with a little wooden box. Since his return, he seems to be living in a strange dream. He has become furtive, and sly, with dangerous and sinister moods, and has even been seen crouching and crawling. One night his daughter awoke to see her father's face pressed against the window of her second-floor bedroom. However, when he's not in a queer fit, he seems to have more energy and vitality than ever before. Holmes finds the answer to the mystery in the professor's knuckles, his dog, and his ivy.

Quotable Quote:

Holmes: *"It's surely time that I disappeared into that little farm of my dreams."*

The Adventure of the Sussex Vampire

First Publication:

The Strand Magazine, January 1924

Principal Predicament:

Robert Ferguson shows up at Baker Street, the wreck of a fine athlete whom Watson knew in his prime. His once great frame has fallen in, his hair is now scanty— and why not? His loving wife, the daughter of a Peruvian merchant, has twice been seen assaulting his charming, teenaged son, "a poor little inoffensive cripple," the child of a previous marriage. Her behavior toward her own dear little baby has been even worse; she's bitten his neck and, it would appear, drunk the poor baby's blood. Ferguson has begun to gather information about vampires.

Illustration by Howard K. Elock, 1925.

Notable Feature:

Written during a time that Conan Doyle was immersed in writing and lecturing on spirits and fairies, it is worth noting that his fictional detective adamantly proclaimed, "This Agency stands flat-footed upon the ground and there it must remain. The world is big enough for us. No ghosts need apply."

Oddities and Discrepancies:

Twice in this story Holmes refers to "this Agency." In the original manuscripts the word appeared with a capital "A." What Agency? There is no other reference to Holmes's "Agency" in the Canon although in "The Disappearance of Lady Frances Carfax" there is a passing reference to "Holmes's own small, but very efficient, organization."

The Brooding Bachelor in a World of Women

One thing is certain, Sherlock Holmes could never be branded a "ladies' man." Indeed, some have thought him a Victorian-era misogynist and with good reason. He was inclined to boast of his disdain for women, saying things like, "I am not a whole-souled admirer of womankind," and "Women are never to be entirely trusted—not the best of them."

The great sleuth had to concede that, for him women remained a mys-

tery. "Woman's heart and mind are insoluble puzzles to the male," he complained. With a shrug he told Watson, "The fair sex is your department," and added, "The motives of women are so inscrutable. . . . Their most trivial action may mean volumes, or their most extraordinary conduct may depend upon a hairpin or a curling-tongs."

Holmes shunned intimacy with women, but to be fair, he shunned intimacy with men as well. A procession of ravishing women sought his aid, but Sherlock Holmes remained steadfastly disinterested.

"What a very attractive woman!" I exclaimed, turning to my companion.

He had lit his pipe again and was leaning back with drooping eyelids. "Is she?" he said languidly; "I did not observe."

"I did not observe." This coming from Sherlock Holmes—a man who could tell volumes about a person's life from the observation of a pocket watch—is not to be believed. It is sheer bluff on the part of the brooding bachelor.

On at least two occasions his mask of disinterest slipped. There was, of course, **Irene Adler,** a dainty opera singer and adventuress and the only woman to outwit the master detective. How could he not admire her? According to Watson:

> To Sherlock Holmes she is always *the* woman. I have seldom heard him mention her under any other name. In his eyes she eclipses and predominates the whole of her sex. It was not that he felt any emotion akin to love for Irene Adler. All emotions, and that one particularly, were abhorrent to his cold, precise but admirably balanced mind. . . . And yet there was but one woman to him.

At the end of his carer, after his retirement to Sussex, Sherlock Holmes encountered one other woman who took his breath away—**Maud Bellamy** of Fulworth. In a rare admission, Holmes made this note in his case book:

> Women have seldom been an attraction for me, for my brain has always governed my heart, but I could not look upon her perfect clear-cut face, with all the soft freshness of the downlands in her delicate coloring, without realizing that no young man would cross her path unscathed.

Both Holmes and Watson may have overlooked the obvious when it came to "the woman" at the center of Sherlock's life. Without a doubt, his most satisfying relationship with the opposite sex was with **Mrs. Hudson** (move over Irene).

He depended on the landlady with the "stately tread" for her daily attention, efficiency, and assistance. She, in return, adored him. A surrogate mother who worried and fussed over her tenant, Mrs. Hudson endured his untidiness, strange callers, and occasional indoor revolver practice. Though the detective was "the very worst tenant in London," Mrs. Hudson "stood in the deepest awe of him and never dared to interfere with him, however outrageous his proceedings might seem."

Holmes coped with feelings of tenderness by imagining his female clients as kin. Pondering the dilemma of **Violet Hunter** who's been told she would be paid well as governess if only she would cut her hair and sit where ordered,

Holmes mused, "I confess that it is not the situation which I should like to see a sister of mine apply for." And of **Violet de Merville** Holmes waxed compassionate: "I was sorry for her, Watson. I thought of her for the moment as I would have thought of a daughter of my own."

For all his gruff talk, the loner had a good heart. Watson noted Holmes's ability to reassure and calm the frightened women who sought his counsel. "He had an almost hypnotic power of soothing when he wished." After years of observation, the faithful Watson, generous to a fault, came to the conclusion that his friend "disliked and distrusted the sex, but he was always a chivalrous opponent." If nothing else, Holmes was a gentleman.

Aloof and alone, the unsociable sleuth nevertheless was fascinated by the petty dramas of human experience. Wrapped in his dressing gown, he religiously clipped the newspapers' "agony columns" and pasted them into a scrapbook. From this habit of reading the vulgar tidbits, Holmes was well acquainted with the heartbreaks and hardships unique to women. In spite of himself, he worried about the plight of single or widowed women alone in a man's world, like **Violet Smith:**

> "It is part of the settled order of Nature that such a girl should have followers," said Holmes, as he pulled at his meditative pipe, "but for choice not on bicycles in lonely country roads."

Another lone woman who aroused Holmes's concern was **Lady Carfax:**

> One of the most dangerous classes in the world is the drifting and friendless woman. She is the most harmless and often the most useful of mortals, but she is the inevitable inciter of crime in others. She is helpless. . . . She is a stray chicken in a world of foxes. When she is gobbled up she is hardly missed.

Holmes lamented the plight of married women who often had to "submit to be caressed by bloody hands and lecherous lips." The detecting duo listened sympathetically to the Victorian victims of domestic violence. In one case, Holmes sought the assistance of a woman whose life had been ruined, **Kitty Winter.** Doing her part, Kitty tried to warn an endangered bride-to-be:

> I am his last mistress. I am one of a hundred that he has tempted and used and ruined and thrown into the refuse heap, as he will you also. Your refuse heap is more likely to be a grave. . . . If you marry this man he'll be the death of you one way or the other.

Another terrified woman had the bad luck to be married to Captain Peter Carey. A Puritan, whaler, and drunkard, he had been known, "to drive his wife and daughter out of doors in the middle of the night and flog them through the park until the whole village outside the gates was aroused by their screams." Other women, like **Emilia Lucca,** told of being abducted or attacked by men.

> Gorgiano . . . spoke much to me; and

even when his words were to my husband those terrible, glaring, wild-beast eyes of his were always turned upon me. One night his secret came out. I had awakened what he called "love" within him–the love of a brute–a savage. Gennaro had not yet returned when he came. He pushed his way in, seized me in his mighty arms, hugged me in his bear's embrace, covered me with kisses, and implored me to come away with him. I was struggling and screaming when Gennaro entered and attacked him.

Distressed women, each more beautiful than the last, presented their dilemmas to the bachelor detective in the hope of moving him to action. A disproportionate number of them were tall and "queenly," though, to his credit, Holmes also came to the aid of women who were not rich and beautiful. There was placid-faced **Susan Cushing,** a spinster with "grizzled hair," and the mutilated, veiled woman whose suffering inspired Holmes to stretch out his arm and pat her hand. "Poor girl! The ways of fate are indeed hard to understand. If there is not some compensation hereafter, then the world is a cruel jest." Perhaps the most pathetic victim of male cruelty, one who could not be helped, was the deserted **Mary Sutherland,** described as a large woman with a heavy fur boa round her neck, a preposterous hat, and a vacuous face.

The exotic and passionate women in Holmes's world were sometimes of Spanish descent, as was **Isadora Klein,** *"the* celebrated beauty. There was never a woman to touch her. She is pure Spanish, the real blood of the masterful Conquistadors." Another hot-blooded beauty was **Maria Pinto,** originally from Brazil, "rare and wonderful in her beauty. It was a deep rich nature, too, passionate, whole-hearted, tropical."

Not all the ladies were of the leisure class. Holmes's cases frequently involved working women—cooks, serving girls, waiting maids, scullery maids, and nurses. At least five distraught women who sought Holmes's aid worked as governesses.

The maids he met were a mixed batch. **Susan Stockdale** had secured employment as a maid, albeit a dishonest one. When Holmes discovered her eavesdropping, he seized her by the shoulder and dragged her into the room. She "entered with ungainly struggle like some huge awkward chicken, torn,

squawking, out of its coop." Holmes was not sympathetic, "Just a little wheezy, Susan, are you not? You breathe too heavily." **Theresa Wright,** a maid from Australia, was faithful to Lady Brackenstall, her "bonny bird." Though described as taciturn, suspicious, and ungracious, she was devoted to her mistress whom she had nursed as a baby. Her steady hand still soothed the Lady's brow.

Another housemaid, the unfortunate **Agatha,** is remembered as the only woman ever seriously wronged by Sherlock Holmes. In order to save Lady Blackwell from blackmail, Holmes disguised himself as a plumber and courted the unsuspecting maid. "I'm engaged," Holmes blithely confessed to Watson, explaining that he needed information. "Surely you have gone too far!" protested Watson. "It was a most necessary step," Holmes replied matter-of-factly. "But the girl, Holmes?" To which Holmes just "shrugged his shoulders." Tsk, tsk.

One housekeeper named **Martha** assisted the great detective in capturing a secret agent. Described as "a dear old ruddy-faced woman in a country cap," Martha stroked a black cat and fooled a Mr. Von Bork with her "air of comfortable somnolence."

The solitary sleuth often generalized about the ways of womankind, but he was also capable of rejecting societal stereotypes. Even he had to admit that women, like men, were capable of the full range of human behavior, though perhaps he overstated the case when he said to Watson, "I assure you that the most winning woman I ever knew was hanged for poisoning three little children for their insurance money."

A Glossary of Holmesian Victoriana

—⚬⚬⚬—

agony column–personal advertisements in English newspapers; Holmes used them to good effect in *The Sign of the Four* and "The Adventure of the Blue Carbuncle," among other stories.

The Assizes–superior courts in every English county that met periodically to handle major civil and criminal cases; mentioned in a number of stories in the Canon; less serious matters were handled by local Justices of the Peace.

baronet–hereditary rank just below the nobility; Sir Charles Baskerville (*The Hound of the Baskervilles*) was a baronet; see Orders of Precedence, p. 172.

the boots–servant who cleaned and polished boots and shoes nightly.

Blue–designation of varsity athlete from Oxford and Cambridge; mentioned in "The Adventure of the Three Students."

Blues–nickname for one of the regiments of cavalry that guarded the Sovereign.

blue ribbon–sign of a temperance organization, worn to indicate membership/sobriety, as by Jim Browner in "The Adventure of the Cardboard Box."

Bradshaw–railway guide for the British Isles; railways were then private and relatively unregulated, with constantly changing service; Holmes consults Bradshaw's before leaving on many of the adventures that take place outside of Greater London.

brougham–a carriage.

bull's-eye–a kind of lantern with a focused beam; Holmes uses one in *The Sign of the Four,* among other stories.

commissionaire–a uniformed doorman, guide, or messenger, generally a retired soldier.

crib–home, residence; part of nineteenth century criminal slang in both England and the U.S. rediscovered by "gangster" rappers in the late twentieth; in Victorian slang, by extension a job or situation; found in "The Adventure of the Stock-Broker's Clerk," "The Adventure of the Reigate Squires," "The Red-Headed League."

colonel–the person who commanded the principal unit of the British army in the nineteenth century, the regiment, which was composed of up to 1,000 men. Colonel Barclay, who died in "The Adventure of the Crooked Man," was commander of his regiment, in which he had started as a private. Such an event, uncommon but not unheard of in the American army, was remarkable in the very traditional and rigidly stratified British army.

consumption–tuberculosis, a staple of nineteenth century literature and a major health problem at the time.

coronet–a kind of crown worn by members of the nobility who were not necessarily part of the Royal Family.

crown–a coin worth five shillings, or one-quarter of a pound.

doctor–in Holmes's time, a physician, one who dealt with and prescribed for internal problems; surgeons, who were lower in status, dealt with broken bones and external wounds; physicians were addressed as "Dr.," while surgeons had to do with "Mr." In *The Hound of the Baskervilles,* Holmes addressed his visitor as Doctor. "Mister, sir, Mister–a humble M.R.C.S." (member of the Royal College of Surgeons), replied Mr. Mortimer.

dog cart–a two-wheel open cart originally built with a back seat that folded into a box to hold dogs, not a vehicle built for dogs to pull; Holmes notices from the pattern of the mud splashes on her coat that Miss Helen Stoner of "The Adventure of the Speckled Band" had ridden in one on her way in from the country. "There is no vehicle save a dog-cart which throws up mud in that way."

downs–rolling uplands in southeast England, from an Old English word that also gave us *dune.*

entail–English law that allowed an heir to use the income from an estate, but not to sell or otherwise dispose of the land itself; "breaking" an entail is an issue behind "The Adventure of the Priory School."

foolscap–a kind of writing paper, originally so called because it bore the watermark of a fool's cap; Mr. Jabez Wilson copies the *Encyclopaedia Britannica* on it in "The Red-Headed League."

four-in-hand–a coach pulled by four horses.

gaiters–leggings worn on the street to keep the trousers clean; Lord Robert St. Simon, the noble bachelor of the story of the same name, wore them; Watson described his dress as "careful to the verge of foppishness."

growler–a four-wheel cab, said to have taken its name from the sound of its steel wheels on the street.

hansom–a two-wheel cab, faster and more maneuverable than a growler, but able to take only two passengers.

Honorable–a courtesy title for members of Parliament and the children of some nobles. The Honorable Ronald Adair was a victim in "The Adventure of the Empty House."

hunting crop–a whip used by horsemen. Holmes's favorite weapon was a *loaded* hunting crop, its handle weighted with iron, as evidenced in "The Adventure of the Six Napoleons" and "The Red-Headed League."

Lady–a courtesy title for the wives and daughters of nobles. Lady Frances Carfax of the story of that name was "the sole survivor of the direct family of the late Earl of Rufton"; Mary Fraser of Adelaide, Australia, became Lady

Brackenstall, wife of Sir Eustace, in "The Adventure of the Abbey Grange."

landau–a kind of carriage with a roof divided in two, so that half could be open or closed.

laudanum–opium mixed with alcohol.

lens–magnifying glass; for Holmes an essential tool for crime detection.

life preserver–a short bludgeon loaded with lead; a blackjack; a common weapon of criminals in Victorian London, one was used to kill young Cadogan West in "The Bruce-Partington Plans."

plate–eating utensils of silver and gold; one way in which rich households in the nineteenth century both kept and displayed their wealth; it was normally part of the butler's job to secure the family plate, which was a frequent target of housebreakers.

pound–English currency, worth about $5 in Holmes's time. See Pounds to pence . . ., page tk.

shag–a kind of tobacco.

shilling–a coin worth one-twentieth of a pound, or about 25 cents U.S. in Holmes's time; members of the Baker Street Irregulars were paid a shilling a day when on duty.

singlestick–a wooden stick used to train swordsmen.

trap–a light carriage.

The Adventure of the Three Garridebs

First Publication:

Collier's, October 1924

Principal Predicament:

John Garrideb, an American in London, shows up at Holmes's door on a peculiar mission. An American real estate tycoon, Alexander Hamilton Garrideb, was proud of the "queerness" of his name, to the extent that he left a will stipulating that his vast estate be divided among three men with the surname "Garrideb"–if three such people could be found in the world. Holmes's visitor, eager to inherit his share of the fortune, has already scoured the Americas, to no avail. Now his treasure hunt has led him to London. Holmes is not fooled for a moment. After the chubby-faced American has left, Holmes removes the pipe from his lips and muses aloud, "I was wondering, Watson, what on earth could be the object of this man telling us such a rigmarole of lies."

Notable Features:

(1) Watson is able to date this case June 1902 because it was the same month that Holmes refused a knighthood. (2) Watson also records a memorable moment in his own life, when Holmes expresses concern after Watson is shot in the thigh. "It was worth a wound–it was worth many wounds–to know the depth of loyalty and love which lay behind that cold mask. The clear, hard eyes were dimmed for a moment, and the firm lips were shaking. For the one and only time I caught a glimpse of a great heart as well as of a great brain."

"My friend took the instrument and I heard the usual syncopated dialogue." Illustration by Howard K. Elcock.

The Adventure of the Illustrious Client

First Publication:

Collier's, November 1924

Principal Predicament:

The icy and infatuated Violet de Merville has accepted the marriage pro-posal of the fiendish but handsome Baron Gruner, and she will not listen to rea-son. Holmes, persuaded by Sir James Damery, acting on behalf of an unnamed client, is both intrigued by the prospect of matching wits with "a real aristocrat of crime" and sympathetic to preventing what will surely be a tragic union. He does his best, going in person to plead and bargain with the villain, to no avail. He then visits the bride-to-be, taking with him the plainspoken Kitty Winter, whose life has been ruined by the Baron. In what Holmes later describes to Watson as the meeting of flame and ice, Winter tells de Merville, "If you marry this man he'll be the death of you one way or the other." The warning falls on deaf ears, though it is not without consequence. Two days after this interview, Watson stops dead in his tracks in front of the one-legged newsvender's plac-ard, when he sees the awful headline "murderous attack upon Sherlock Holmes."

Notable Features:

We never actually learn the identity of the "illustrious client" nor does he appear in the story line. Also, in this tale Conan Doyle contemplates some of the issues facing Victorian women who were vulnerable to male violence in the days before battered women's shelters and who could be forced into a life of prostitution if their reputations were ruined.

Oddities and Discrepancies:

As the story opens, Holmes and Watson are at a Turkish bath, lying side by side on couches in a drying room (where Watson finds Holmes "more human than anywhere else"). Holmes reaches for a paper in the pocket of his coat "which hung beside him." Why did Holmes have his coat in the drying room?

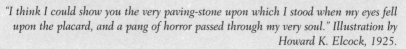

"I think I could show you the very paving-stone upon which I stood when my eyes fell upon the placard, and a pang of horror passed through my very soul." Illustration by Howard K. Elcock, 1925.

The Adventure of the Three Gables

First Publication:

Liberty, September 1926

Principal Predicament:

Mrs. Maberley, a refined, elderly woman, still in mourning from the death of her dashing son in Rome a month earlier, has been offered a high price for her house, on the condition that she walk out with just the clothes on her back. Holmes confers with Langdale Pike, "his human book of reference upon all matters of social scandal"–who fills him in on the latest gossip, but, before Holmes can act, the Maberley house is burglarized. Nothing of value seems to be missing. However, in a struggle with Mrs. Maberley the thieves drop what appears to be the last page of a novel. With that, Holmes knows the whole story.

Notable Feature:

This story has generated discussion of remarks made by Holmes that seem racist to our modern sensibility.

Quotable Quote:

Holmes: *"You can't play with edged tools forever without cutting those dainty hands."*

The Adventure of the Blanched Soldier

First Publication:

Liberty, October 1926

Principal Predicament:

In the days following the Boer War, James Dodd is desperate to find his wartime friend, Godfrey Emsworth. In his search he has interviewed everyone from Godfrey's old nurse to his mousey little mother. The father claims that Godfrey has gone on a voyage round the world and can't be reached, but James doesn't buy the story, especially not after Ralph the butler ran from his questioning in tears. Is Godfrey dead? Has he gotten mixed up in some criminal activity? As James was pondering all this, he looked up and saw the young man in question–as pale as a ghost. It left James with a feeling of horror, but with no less determination to get to the truth.

Notable Feature:

This story is told by Holmes in the first person, sans Watson.

Illustration by Frederic Dorr Steele for Liberty *Magazine, October 16, 1926.*

The Unchronicled Cases of Sherlock Holmes: A Crossword Puzzle

—◊◊◊—

Throughout Watson's narratives are references to numerous cases handled by Sherlock Holmes which remain untold. See if you can complete the titles of these "unchronicled" cases. The stories in which they are mentioned are in parentheses after the clues.

Across:

1. The famous _____ Scandal of the Nonpareil Club. (*Hound of the Baskervilles*)
2. Affair of the Vatican _____ (which Holmes investigated on behalf of the Pope). (*Hound*)
3. The Camberwell _____ Case (Holmes examined the victim's watch.) (*Five Orange Pips*)
7. The Bishop _____ Jewel Case. (*Sign of the Four*)
8. The "Bogus" _____ Affair. (*Cardboard Box*)
9. Theft of the Black _____ of the Borgias. (*Six Napoleons*)
10. Dr. Moore _____[']_____ dramatic introduction to Holmes was never recounted by Watson. (*Devil's Foot*)
12. The Adventure of the _____ Captain. (*Naval Treaty*)
13. The Case of Victor Lynch, the _____. (*Sussex Vampire*)
14. The repulsive story of the _____ _____ [2 words]. (*Golden Pince-Nez*)
16. The Case of Ricoletti, who had an abominable wife and a _____-_____. (*Musgrave Ritual*)
19. A story for which the world is not yet prepared. The _____ _____ _____ _____ [4 words]. (*Sussex Vampire*)

20. The Case of Vamberry, the wine _____. (*Musgrave Ritual*)
22. The Problem of the Grosvenor Square Furniture _____. (*Noble Bachelor*)
23. The Adventure of the Old Russian _____. (*Musgrave Ritual*)
25. The Case of Vittoria, the _____ belle. (*Sussex Vampire*)
27. The Adventure of the Paradol _____. (*Five Orange Pips*)
28. The _____ House Case, solved by Sherlock Holmes without the help of his brother Mycroft. (*Greek Interpreter*)

Down:

1. The Case of the Two _____ Patriarchs. (*Retired Colourman*)
2. Holmes arrested Wilson, the notorious _____ trainer. (*Black Peter*)
4. The Singular Adventure of the Grice Patersons in the _____ _____ _____ [3 words]. (*Five Orange Pips*)
5. Holmes exposed the atrocious conduct of Colonel Upwood in connection with the scandal at the _____ Club. [see 1 across] (*Hound*)
6. Holmes saved Major Prendergast in the Tankerville Club _____. (*Five Orange Pips*)
7. The Case of the Venomous Lizard or _____. (*Sussex Vampire*)

11. The Amateur Mendicant _____.
    (*Five Orange Pips*)
15. Watson threatened to reveal to the
    world the details of the politician,
    the lighthouse, and the trained
    _____. (*Veiled Lodger*)
16. The Singular Affair of the
    Aluminum _____. (*Musgrave
    Ritual*)
17. The Case of Colonel Warburton's
    _____, introduced to Holmes by
    Watson. (*Engineer's Thumb*)
18. Holmes had a commission from the
    _____ of Turkey. (*Blanched Soldier*)

21. At the express desire of the Pope,
    Holmes investigated the death of
    Cardinal _____. (*Black Peter*)
24. _____, the Hammersmith wonder,
    a case filed under "V" in Holmes's
    index. (*Sussex Vampire*)
26. Journalist/duelist Isadora Persano
    was found mad with a matchbox
    containing a remarkable _____,
    said to be unknown to science.
    (*Problem of Thor Bridge*)

***Solutions to the crossword puzzle
may be found on page 216***

Filling Our Homes with Holmes:
Memorabilia Honoring the Master Detective

———✑∿∿∿✑———

Sherlock Holmes exists for most of us as if he were a fact of nature, like the air we breathe, immediately recognizable. *The Oxford English Dictionary* lists his given name as a verb meaning "to make deductions about, to assess, to deduce." Alive and well in the public imagination, he is not relegated to the past, but transcends the boundaries of Victorian London. A poster in the New York City subway shows him reading a paper while riding alongside other straphangers. His face is an icon in telephone yellow pages and on anti-crime neighborhood watch signs, alerting ordinary sleuths to phone the police if they see something suspicious. Holmes belongs to us all.

In *A Sherlock Holmes Handbook,* Christopher Redmond observed:

> Sherlock Holmes, who was conceived on a page of Arthur Conan Doyle's notebook and brought to birth in a shilling paperback, has escaped his creator's control. Surviving embarrassing distortions by advertisers and film directors, surviving parodies and caricatures, the decay of time and the damage of dog-eared pages, he has earned eternal life.

And so it would seem, from the sheer variety of the available paraphernalia.

Plugs and Dottles, Stuff and Things

Several companies exist to promote the commerce of Sherlock Holmes artifacts, including **The Sherlock Holmes Memorabilia Company,** located in London, **Classic Specialties** of Cincinnati, Ohio, which publishes a *Sherlockian Times* catalog, and **The Baker Street Emporium** in Seal Beach, California.

Such companies ensure that Sherlockian souvenirs can be had if the price is right. There are things canonical, such as a magnifying glass with a Sherlock Holmes silhouette hand-carved from the cherrywood handle, and pipes of all shapes and sizes, some with bowls in the detective's likeness, smoke literally rising from his deerstalker.

Basil Rathbone Life Mask available from the Baker Street Emporium.

Logo of the Sherlock Holmes Memorabilia Company. By kind permission of The Sherlock Holmes Memorabilia Company, 230 Baker Street, London NW1 5RT, England.

There are lighters engraved with a Holmesian logo and a variety of tobaccos bearing his name.

There is a world of key chains and lapel pins, many bearing the logos of the various Sherlockian societies. One clever pin is the 221-B Door Knocker with a tiny knocker that really moves.

Ceramic collectibles such as commemorative mugs and plates are issued for anniversaries connected with the Canon. One limited edition plate featured portraits of the many actors who have played Holmes and Watson. Other ceramics include an array of busts, figurines, and wall plaques. There's a tea pot in the likeness of a deerstalkered Holmes, with a handle coming out of one ear opposite a spout growing from his neck. And there's a tea cozy, a replica of 221-B Baker Street, with white window panes and a wood-grained door appliquéd onto a brick-printed fabric. The detective peers from one window.

The Holmes/Watson pairing lends itself to reproduction as salt and pepper shakers and bookends. There are lamps, too, like the Hound of the Baskervilles Fan Lamp, an accent light depicting the infamous canine poised to pounce, silhouetted against a full moon, and The Lodgers of 221-B Leaded Glass Lamp featuring silk-screened likenesses of the doctor and detective on art glass with colorful hand-leaded accents in stained glass.

There are holiday ornaments, like the wood carving of an Indian Swamp Adder slithering down Helen Stoner's dummy bell pull and a deerstalker carved from beechwood.

In the realm of the unusual is the Basil Rathbone Life Mask and in the realm of the exquisite, the travel alarm shaped like a Victorian-era pocket watch with the embossed likeness of Sherlock Holmes on its lid.

There are an abundance of sweat shirts, T-shirts and neckties embroidered with Holmesian logos, as well as capes, deerstalkers, book bags, and sweaters.

Then too, there are the paper products, postcards, stationery, note cards, and greeting cards, many featuring the Paget illustrations first published in *The Strand Magazine*. There are rubber stamps (one bearing the words, "I'd rather be at 221-B Baker Street") and wax seals.

For philatelists, there are commemorative postage stamps honoring the Conan Doyle stories issued from a range of countries, including Nicaragua and Australia. In 1992, St. Vincent of the Grenadines, a Caribbean island, issued a series of stamps depicting scenes from the Disney animated movie, *The Great Mouse Detective*. In 1993, Great Britain issued a set of five 24p stamps, 100 years after the publication of the story that rocked the empire describing Holmes's struggle with Moriarty at Reichenbach Falls. Each stamp depicted different canonical adventures– "Reigate Squires," *The Hound of the Baskervilles,* "Six Napoleons," "The Greek

> "There is no branch of detective science which is so important and so much neglected as the art of tracing footsteps."
> —*A Study in Scarlet*

Interpreter," and "The Final Problem."

As early as 1904 there were Sherlock Holmes playing cards. Games are still a big item and include not only a variety of card and board games but elegant chess sets featuring a whole cast of characters. Generally, in recognition of their competing talents, the powerful pieces are designated as Holmes and Moriarty, while Watson is consigned to pieces capable of less potent moves.

There are deerstalkered stuffed toy animals in the shape of cuddly teddy bears and cartoonish dogs; menus and beer coasters from Sherlockian restaurants; golf towels and pocket watches; movie posters and Sherlockian playbills.

For the computer literate, there is the Sherlockian "Mouse" Pad, with a pale blue silhouette of Holmes examining his computer screen through a magnifying glass, and an "Abominable Wife" Screen Saver (a reference to an unchronicled case mentioned in "The Musgrave Ritual").

Serious Collectors of Serious Things

John Bennett Shaw (1913–94) was a Sherlockian scholar, big-hearted advocate for enthusiasts young and old, and "completist" collector. Some said he had "the selectivity of a vacuum cleaner," and even he was heard to jest, "I try to get everything, but I don't have to like it."

Shaw's zeal led to his accumulation of books and items related to the

Canon, a collection the likes of which this world has rarely seen. It is said he kept a picture of Moriarty on the seat of his toilet and a chocolate Sherlockian bunny in his freezer. He even had a collection of Sherlockian panties. But prized in his collection, which included over 10,000 Sherlock Holmes books and pamphlets, were four publications printed in Germany in the 1890s which may have once belonged to the Czarina of Russia.

Completist collectors attempt to acquire a copy of everything that touches on Holmes. Renowned for his Sherlockian collection was James Bliss Austin of Pittsburgh. After his death, his collection was sold to Pepper & Stern for $151,000.

A current collector of note is Peter Blau of Washington, D.C. In addition to actively building his collection, he publishes a newsletter titled *Scuttlebutt from the Spermaceti Press* and maintains a complete list of Sherlock Holmes societies around the world.

Kiyoshi Tanaka is a Japanese Sherlockian whose collection of Holmes memorabilia formed the basis of a 1994 Sherlock Holmes exhibition in Tokyo. Asked how he could afford such items as first editions of the Canon, he joked, "I don't tell my wife how much it cost." The Tokyo exhibit featured everything from signed letters by Arthur Conan Doyle to ticket stubs for Sherlockian movies and events, dolls, pipes, pins, and badges, and an exquisitely rendered miniature of 221-B Baker Street.

So Many Books, So Little Time

According to some estimates, there are more than 7,000,000 copies of hard-cover books about Sherlock Holmes and some 100,000,000 paperbacks, with translations into more than sixty languages. An extensive bibliography of writings about Sherlock Holmes was compiled by Ronald De Waal and completists still use the De Waal publication as a measure of completeness. According to a foreign language Sherlockian collector, Donald Pollock, however, "There's something satisfying about finding a volume that is 'Not in De Waal,' as book dealers might say." German and Spanish translations are easy to find, Yiddish or Afrikaans, a real challenge. Though not exactly "foreign language," it can be exciting to discover a Sherlock Holmes story in Braille or in Gregg shorthand.

Foreign-language editions are collected, not only for the appeal of the exotic alphabets but for the often vivid cover art rendered in bold colors.

While some "completists" collect any books about Sherlock Holmes, others focus on one area of interest. Some collect only editions of one story. Pollock, quoted above, concentrates on editions of *The Hound of the Baskervilles*. "*Hound* is the one thing I actively seek out, catalogue, savor, and regret when a particularly nice copy slips through my grasp. . . . The *Hound* has been published in enough editions and variants to satisfy a collector."

Another collector, Don Hobbs, is hunting translations in the sixty-two languages he claims the Canon can be found in, and formed The Maniac Collectors as an international trading society whose members swap Sherlockian books from around the globe. He wrote, "Once I bought a set of

震動世界五十二件大探案　1

福爾摩斯　冒險史

柯南道爾原著　　夏新　譯

Sherlock Holmes with Watson on the cover of a Chinese-language edition of stories by Conan Doyle.

twelve Chinese editions and had a person at work translate the titles for me. He was able to read eleven out of the twelve. Chinese is a phonetic language and some of the titles were 'Research in Red' (*A Study in Scarlet*) and my favorite, 'The Police Officer Who Was Not Feeling Very Well' (Dying Detective)."

The Adventure of the Lion's Mane

First Publication:

Liberty, November 1926

Principal Predicament:

On a beautiful morning after a storm, the retired detective sets out for a walk and is delighted to meet his neighbor. The two have barely exchanged greetings when they catch sight of young McPherson, staggering like a drunken man. The man falls to the ground in agony and dies screaming, "the Lion's Mane." On his back, Holmes finds raw red welts as if the man had been flogged by a thin wire scourge. Holmes searches the beach, but finds no one who could have done such a thing. Nor does he suspect that McPherson ever took that last swim; his towel is dry. Ian Murdoch hovers around the scene of the crime and is the number one suspect. But then, McPherson's dog dies right at the place where his master had died, and Murdoch screams for opium. This prompts Holmes to remember something he had read long ago.

Notable Feature:

This story is written in first person by the retired Sherlock Holmes.

Oddities and Discrepancies:

McPherson's towel was dry because, in the last moments of his life he didn't take the time to dry off. Why didn't Holmes notice that the dead man was wet?

Illustration by Howard K. Elock for the Strand *Magazine, December 1926.*

The Adventure of
the Retired Colourman

First Publication:

Liberty, December 1926

Principal Predicament:

After a life of ceaseless grind, sixty-one-year-old Josiah Amberley retired from his position as junior partner of Brickfall and Amberley, manufacturers of artistic materials. He bought a little house and settled down with a lovely wife, twenty years younger than himself. Two years later, he arrives at Baker Street, seemingly a broken and miserable creature. He wants help finding his wife who has run off, he says, with both his savings and his chess partner, a young doctor. Watson begins the investigation and is immediately struck by how rundown the man's house is. "How any decent woman could have tolerated such a state of things, I don't know," he says. Mr. Amberley has just begun to improve his old house. He's painting the hallway. Holmes thinks the timing is strange for such a project, but the good doctor accepts Mr. Amberley's reason: "One must do something to ease an aching heart."

Notable Feature:

There is a telephone in the Baker Street flat, a fact that has been noted in two other adventures. In this story, Holmes seems more comfortable than Watson at using the phone. Watson still thinks of the telegraph first.

Quotable Quote:

Holmes: *"Burglary has always been an alternative profession had I cared to adopt it."*

Oddities and Discrepancies:

Holmes suggests that the police will find an indelible pencil on the body. The question is, why would a dying person who loses consciousness halfway through scribbling a short sentence, put the pencil in a pocket? Would the murderer have picked up the pencil and put it neatly in the deceased's pocket? Either scenario is absurd. In fact, the editors of *Liberty* deleted the words "on the body" from their version of the story.

"On that particular evening old Amberley, wishing to give his wife a treat, had taken two upper circle seats at the Haymarket Theatre. At the last moment she had complained of a headache and had refused to go. He had gone alone." Credit: Radio Times Hulton Picture Library

The Adventure of the Veiled Lodger

First Publication:

Liberty, January 1927

Principal Predicament:

For seven years, Eugenia Ronder has lived quietly behind her veil. But lately, her landlady has
been hearing screams in the night from the mysterious lady who seems to be wasting away–screams of
"You cruel beast!" and "Murder!" When the landlady
offers to call the police or the clergy, the tenant
reacts with alarm. But, she laments, it would ease
her mind "if someone knew the truth before I died."
The women agree that the famous detective,
Sherlock Holmes, would serve as the perfect confi-
dante. The veiled lodger instructs her landlady to fetch Holmes, saying, "If he
won't come, tell him I am the wife of Ronder's wild beast show. Say that, and
give him the name Abbas Parva." Holmes perks up at this reference to an
unsolved mystery seven years earlier when the circus had stopped at Abbas
Parva. The whole camp was awakened around midnight by the roars of a lion
and a woman's screams. Moments later, a crowd gathered around the body of
the dead circus owner. Near the cage, Mrs. Ronder lay on her back with the
lion crouching over her. Leonardo, the strong man, and Griggs, the clown, had
driven the lion back into its cage, but not before it had ripped Mrs. Ronder's
face to shreds. How it had gotten loose was an unsolved mystery, as was the reason for the mutilated woman's screams of "Coward! Coward!" Holmes is eager
to hear the explanation offered by the circus woman who has become like a
beast in a cage.

Notable Feature:

This is the shortest story in the Canon and one in which Holmes does no
detecting. However, he is moved to deep sympathy and to great admiration of
the victim's courage.

Quotable Quote:

Holmes: *"The ways of fate are indeed hard to understand. If there is not some
compensation hereafter, then the world is a cruel jest."*

CAPSULE

The Adventure of
Shoscombe Old Place

First Publication:

Liberty, March 1927

Principal Predicament:

According to Watson, who claims in this story to spend half his "wound pension" on racing, Sir Robert Norberton, owner of a racehorse training center, has the reputation of being a dangerous man–"a boxer, an athlete, a plunger on the turf, a lover of fair ladies, and, by all accounts, so far down Queer Street that he may never find his way back again." When Norberton's head trainer shows up at Baker Street, he reports that his employer seems to have changed for the worse; he's stopped sleeping, his eyes are wild, and his behavior toward his sister, Lady Beatrice, has been alarming. He has given away her pet spaniel that she loved as if it were her child. Lady Beatrice has changed too, according to the horse trainer. She's brooding and drinking. But, what the horse trainer really wants to know is why his master has been visiting the old church crypt at night and who is the man who meets him there?

Notable Feature:

This was the last Sherlock Holmes story published.

Quotable Quote:

Holmes: *"Dogs don't make mistakes."*

Illustration by Frank Wiles for the Strand Magazine, *April 1927.*

My Brother, the Consulting Detective

By Mycroft Holmes
(Late of Her Majesty's Government)

Thanks to the efforts of Dr. John H. Watson, the people of Great Britain were surprised to discover late in the last century that in their midst was a new phenomenon, the world's first consulting detective, a man of impeccable insight and compelling intellectual gifts.

Since that time his fame has spread through the world, and his exploits have astonished millions. Yet no one was more astonished by the rise of Sherlock Holmes than the people who knew him best in his youth. From Reverend Witherspoon, Rector of St. Athanasius in our quiet rural county, to Mr. Pitiless, our tutor, and even Grimes, our gamekeeper, Sherlock was "the strange 'un."

It was not exactly that he was a bad boy. Yet virtually no one (with the possible exception of himself—modesty was never his vice) felt him destined for greatness.

While avid enough at those matters he found interesting—from tobacco ash to footprints—he treated whole areas of learning with a dismissive contempt. His knowledge of Latin was sketchy, of Greek ludicrous, of rhetoric and philosophy so unscientific as to be all but useless.

His natural sciences were somewhat better. He was more than a passable chemist and might have made a physician if he had properly disciplined himself. But he left tutors and dons in despair as he embarked unbidden and unled into arcane areas of inquiry, before setting himself up in a "profession" that no gentleman could respectably pursue.

I cast my lot with the study of broad patterns of economic and political life, from the bimetallic question to our government of India. Sherlock preferred to focus on the concrete, the individualistic, and—dare I say it?—the banal.

These occasionally provided him with material rewards, a not unwelcome thing since personal reverses had forced our father to leave us with only about a thousand pounds a year.

Fairness compels me to report that he was enormously helpful to Their Majesties in a number of cases, including those of the Bruce-Partington Plans, the dispatching of Professor Moriarty, and in frustrating German espionage plans on the eve of the Great War.

But it was strongly felt in Whitehall–and in the Palace–that it was our empire's loss that Sherlock confined his very real gifts too often to tawdry little cases of personal indiscretion, unimportant thievery, or homicide among the barely useful classes. These in the long run brought him only personal satisfaction and a measure of popular renown.

Not that I was jealous of his fame. Contemptuous as I am of the acclaim of the masses, I have not one whit of resentment that it was my younger and less civic-minded brother whose celebrity seems likely to endure.

People often ask when last I heard from my brother. Though we had kept to our own spheres for most of our adult lives, only rarely meeting (and that often in a professional capacity) we grew closer after our respective retirements. He had devoted himself to beekeeping in the Sussex Downs, while I have a cot-tage not far from Dover where I have been working on the definitive study of the Persian satrapy under the reign of Cyrus the VI, a subject that has long occupied my curiosity.

We found ourselves drawn together, and spent many happy hours overlooking the Channel, discussing our respective studies and recalling our careers. From these conversations it is clear to me that Dr. Watson omitted more than he included of my brother's life and works, but a vow of silence compels me to share his reticence on these fascinating subjects.

Despite the untimely deaths of our parents, we come of long-lived stock, and when last we met he announced that he intended to revisit the Tibetan precincts he had frequented following the affair of the Reichenbach Falls, and where he had learned so much from the monks. That was a number of years ago, yet I have no difficulty in believing that he is still there, and that at some point I will hear from him again.

From what I read in today's newspapers, the world has no less need of his skills, and I know that, despite the lure of more serious subjects, detection is, as it were, in his blood.

Story Abbreviations

In 1947, American Sherlockian Jay Finley Christ developed a system of coded abbreviations for each story in the Canon. These abbreviations have been especially useful in scholarly Sherlockian texts and footnotes, in place of the cumbersome story titles. This listing utilizes a shortened title reference after the abbreviation.

ABBE The Abbey Grange
BERY The Beryl Coronet
BLAC Black Peter
BLAN The Blanched Soldier
BLUE The Blue Carbuncle
BOSC The Boscombe Valley Mystery
BRUC The Bruce-Partington Plans
CARD The Cardboard Box
CHAS Charles Augustus Milverton
COPP The Copper Beeches
CREE The Creeping Man
CROO The Crooked Man
DANC The Dancing Men
DEVI The Devil's Foot
DYIN The Dying Detective
EMPT The Empty House
ENGR The Engineer's Thumb

FINA The Final Problem
FIVE The Five Orange Pips
GLOR The "Gloria Scott"
GOLD The Golden Pince-Nez
GREE The Greek Interpreter
HOUN The Hound of the Baskervilles
IDEN A Case of Identity
ILLU The Illustrious Client
LADY Lady Frances Carfax
LAST His Last Bow
LION The Lion's Mane
MAZA The Mazarin Stone
MISS The Missing Three-Quarter
MUSG The Musgrave Ritual
NAVA The Naval Treaty
NOBL The Noble Bachelor
NORW The Norwood Builder
PRIO The Priory School
REDC The Red Circle
REDH The Red-Headed League
REIG The Reigate Squires/Puzzle
RESI The Resident Patient
RETI The Retired Colourman
SCAN A Scandal in Bohemia
SECO The Second Stain
SHOS Shoscombe Old Place
SIGN The Sign of the Four

SILV	Silver Blaze	**3GAB**	The Three Gables
SIXN	The Six Napoleons	**3GAR**	The Three Garridebs
SOLI	The Solitary Cyclist	**3STU**	The Three Students
SPEC	The Speckled Band	**TWIS**	The Man with the Twisted Lip
STOC	The Stock-Broker's Clerk	**VALL**	The Valley of Fear
STUD	A Study in Scarlet	**VEIL**	The Veiled Lodger
SUSS	The Sussex Vampire	**WIST**	Wisteria Lodge
THOR	Thor Bridge	**YELL**	The Yellow Face

Crossword Puzzle Answers

Across:

1. The famous **CARD** Scandal of the Nonpareil Club.
2. Affair of the Vatican **CAMEOS.**
3. The Camberwell **POISONING** Case.
7. The Bishop**GATE** Jewel Case.
8. The "Bogus" **LAUNDRY** Affair.
9. Theft of the Black **PEARL** of the Borgias.
10. Dr. Moore **AGAR[']S** dramatic introduction to Holmes was never recounted by Watson.
12. The Adventure of the **TIRED** Captain.
13. The Case of Victor Lynch, the **FORGER.**
14. The repulsive story of the **RED LEECH**.
16. The Case of Ricoletti, who had an abominable wife and a **CLUBFOOT**.
19. A story for which the world is not yet prepared. The **GIANT RAT OF SUMATRA**.
20. The Case of Vamberry, the wine **MERCHANT.**
22. The Problem of the Grosvenor Square Furniture **VAN.**
23. The Adventure of the Old Russian **WOMAN.**
25. The Case of Vittoria, the **CIRCUS** belle.
27. The Adventure of the Paradol **CHAMBER.**
28. The **MANOR** House Case, solved by Sherlock Holmes without the help of his brother Mycroft.

Down:

1. The Case of the Two **COPTIC** Patriarchs.
2. Holmes arrested Wilson, the notorious **CANARY** trainer.
4. The Singular Adventure of the Grice Patersons in the **ISLAND OF UFFA.**
5. Holmes exposed the atrocious conduct of Colonel Upwood in connection with the scandal at the **NONPAREIL** Club.
6. Holmes saved Major Prendergast in the Tankerville Club **SCANDAL.**
7. The Case of the Venomous Lizard or **GILA.**
11. The Amateur Mendicant **SOCIETY.**
15. Watson threatened to reveal to the world the details of the politician, the lighthouse, and the trained **CORMORANT.**
16. The Singular Affair of the Aluminum **CRUTCH.**
17. The Case of Colonel Warburton's **MADNESS,** introduced to Holmes by Watson.
18. Holmes had a commission from the **SULTAN** of Turkey.
21. At the express desire of the Pope, Holmes investigated the death of Cardinal **TOSCA.**
24. **VIGOR**, the Hammersmith wonder, a case filed under "V" in Holmes's index.
26. Journalist/duelist Isadora Persano was found mad with a matchbox containing a remarkable **WORM,** said to be unknown to science.